DINING TABLES

DINING TABLES

Outstanding Projects from America's Best Craftsmen

WITH PLANS AND COMPLETE INSTRUCTIONS
FOR BUILDING 9 TABLES

KIM CARLETON GRAVES
WITH MASHA ZAGER

The Taunton Press

The Taunton Press
Inspiration for hands-on living™

The Taunton Press, Inc., 63 South Main Street, PO Box 5506, Newtown, CT 06470-5506
e-mail: tp@taunton.com

Distributed by Publishers Group West

INTERIOR DESIGNER: Lori Wendin
LAYOUT ARTIST: Cathy Cassidy
COVER PHOTOS: Dennis Griggs, Rick Miles, Richard Bienkowski
ILLUSTRATOR: Melanie Powell

LIBRARY OF CONGRESS CATALOGING-IN-PUBLICATION DATA
Graves, Kim Carleton.
    Dining tables : outstanding projects from America's best craftsmen : with plans and complete instructions for building 9 tables / Kim Carleton Graves, with Masha Zager.
        p. cm.
    Includes bibliographical references.
    ISBN 1-56158-491-6
    1. Tables. 2. Furniture making. I. Zager, Masha. II. Title.
TT197.5.T3 G73 2002
685.1'3--dc21
                                                                    2001047649

Printed in the United States of America
10 9 8 7 6 5 4 3 2 1

About Your Safety: Working with wood is inherently dangerous. Using hand or power tools improperly or ignoring safety practices can lead to permanent injury or even death. Don't try to perform operations you learn about here (or elsewhere) unless you're certain they are safe for you. If something about an operation doesn't feel right, don't do it. Look for another way. We want you to enjoy the craft, so please keep safety foremost in your mind whenever you're in the shop.

For Natalie Lunn, mentor and friend, who, as technical director of
the Bard College Theater, taught me lessons that I remember and use daily
in my shop more than 20 years later—the great teacher keeps on teaching.
Thanks, Nat.

ACKNOWLEDGMENTS

Writing a book, like most things in life, is a collaborative effort. I'd like to thank
the staff at The Taunton Press, especially my editors, Tom Clark and Helen
Albert, who steered me through this project. Rich Bienkowski, my photographer,
produced the clear and concise photographs. His teaching me how to edit in
the camera frame has been valuable in my own design work. Bill Duckworth
at *Fine Woodworking* sets me straight and points me in the right direction on a
regular basis.

The six talented and generous woodworkers whose tables appear in this book
gave freely of their valuable time and expertise. Thanks also to Robert Allen,
Peter Coe, and the other fine woodworkers whose tables, for one reason or
another, I was unable to use.

My friends and colleagues Neil Verplank of Dovetail Woodworking in
Chicago, Anatoli Lapushner of Anatoli's Restoration in New York, and Darryl
Keil of Vacuum Pressing Systems in Brunswick, Maine, helped in reviewing the
text and providing technical assistance. I owe a special debt to Kirk Schuly of
K.S. Furniture and Design, with whom I share a workspace. He not only con-
tributed the modern round table on p. 140 but also has been an ever-present,
always available teacher, sounding board, second hand, and friend.

Finally, my companion and co-author Masha Zager: While living with someone you love is wonderful, we were warned that trying to write a book together
might not be so wonderful. But writing this book with Masha has been nothing
but great fun. Not only have I learned something about writing, I've also gotten
to spend a lot of time with her as well—something busy couples don't often get a
chance to do. And you, the reader, are the better for it as well. Masha took my
first-draft ramblings and turned them into polished prose. The ideas here are
mine, but the book is hers.

CONTENTS

INTRODUCTION

What could be more essential to a home than a dining table? The table is the "board" in "bed and board," that catchphrase of domesticity. People have been eating at tables for 3,000 years, since they gave up nomadic life for the comforts of home. I suspect the human brain is hardwired to prefer sharing meals with family and friends to hunkering down with takeout food in front of the TV.

Of course, we use our dining-room tables for purposes other than dining. Mine tends to become an extra desk. Others are pressed into service as conference tables, card tables, or work tables. This sort of thing has probably been going on for 3,000 years as well. A good dining table is a versatile piece of furniture.

There's nothing new under the sun. All of the issues in this book are as ancient as the table itself: how to make the table beautiful, how to make it big enough (but not too big), and how to make it strong.

The earliest pictures of tables show elaborate decorations and carvings. The Romans carved table legs in the shapes of animals, both real and imaginary. They made their tables into showpieces, as we continue to do today. The size of dining tables and their role in entertaining guests make them a focus for display.

We also know that people have been worrying for centuries, if not longer, about how to feed a throng. In the Middle Ages, feudal lords just set up extra tables in the dining hall when the odd hundred knights came riding across the plain for a visit. As early as the 15th century, the English invented an expanding table. The "draw table" had three tabletops stacked one on top of another, and the lower two could be pulled out to lengthen the table.

Another preoccupation over the course of history has been keeping tables from collapsing when they were moved or loaded down with food. The trestle table was an early solution to this problem, followed by the stretcher table, and then by apron and pedestal tables.

In this book, I will address all of these issues. The first chapter, Table-Building Basics, provides technical information about sizing tables and about building tables that will survive the stresses of wood movement and of domestic life, and also discusses aesthetic design issues. The nine projects illustrate a range of historical styles, from 17th century through modern, and of solutions to technical problems, as worked out by myself and six other craftsmen. You will find tables that can be knocked down, folded up, and expanded; you will find tables held steady by trestles, pedestal assemblies, cross braces, and aprons.

I've also included a variety of construction techniques—solid wood, veneer over sheet goods, and veneer over a torsion box. Woodworking lore and techniques that are applicable to many of the projects are scattered throughout the book, so it's a good idea to read through the book even if you're only planning to make one or two of the tables.

I hope there is something here for everyone. But if you don't find exactly the table you want to build, use the book as a reference source when you design and build your own table. Even though the problems are old, you can always find new solutions to them. Once you understand the principles of table design and the basic techniques for building, the possibilities for invention are endless.

TABLE-BUILDING BASICS

A table, pared down to its essentials, is just a flat surface raised to an appropriate height for dining. The surface could be held up by legs or a pedestal or, I suppose, could even be hung from the ceiling. In college I made a table out of a large, wooden telephone-cable spool tipped on its side; in the shop I throw a piece of scrap plywood on top of sawhorses at lunchtime. While these last two solutions are simple, neither of them is comfortable or attractive. Making a table that is durable, functional, comfortable to use, and aesthetically pleasing is harder than just making a table.

SIZING THE TABLE

Although you may be tempted to find a design you like and dive right into making sawdust, you should consider first whether the table will accommodate the people who will use it and whether it will fit into the available space.

Sizing for everyday use

How big a table do you need? Two people can't share an intimate dinner at a huge table. A family of six at a small table feels claustrophobic. Do you need to seat two, four, or six on a regular basis? How often do you entertain? When you entertain, how many people do you typically invite? For holidays, does the whole clan come to your house? Do you need to serve 10, 12, or more?

Ergonomic research has established the minimum and optimum space required by diners at a table. You can use the information in "Place Settings" on pp. 6–8 to calculate how big a table you need for every day and for special occasions. In this book, when I say a table "seats four formally" or "seats six informally," I'm using these calculations. That doesn't mean you can't squeeze in another person if you have to. (The information on the place-setting math and clearance comes from *Human Dimension and Interior Space* by Julius Panero and Martin Zelnik [see "Further Reading" on p. 184], an invaluable reference tool for designing furniture.)

In general, the table should be a comfortable fit for the number of people who use it all the time and an adequate fit when a few extra people show up looking hungry. You can always accommodate crowds by making the table expandable.

Seating a crowd

When the crowd descends, you need to expand the size of your table while maintaining its structural integrity. Many solutions to this problem have been developed, the most common being expansion leaves and drop leaves.

Expansion leaves are stored apart from the table. When they are needed, the table is separated into halves using a table slide. The leaves are then dropped into the resulting space and the table is pushed back together.

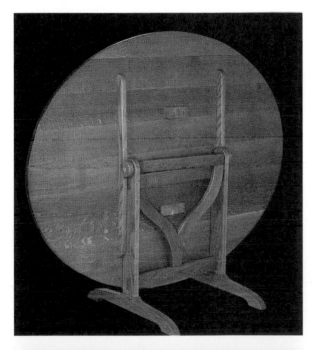

You can keep an extra table in storage for special occasions, left, or design your everyday table to be expandable, above.

Today's table height of 29 in. to 30 in. was not always the standard. This 27⅞-in.-high Shaker trestle table is based on an original in Hancock Shaker Village.

Large tables can be made with modern materials to reduce weight. This table used torsion-box construction and has a satinwood veneer.

Several expansion table projects are included in this book.

Drop leaves, which are raised up and down on hinges attached to the tabletop, come in all shapes and sizes—for example, rectangular leaves on a rectangular table or semicircular leaves on a square table. The disadvantage of using drop leaves on dining tables is that no one can sit in front of a leaf that is in the down position.

With either of these methods, it is relatively easy to expand a table that normally seats four into one that seats six, eight, or even 10 people. If you need even more room, try building a breakdown table like the trestle table shown on p. 40 or a folding table like the vineyard table shown on p. 56 to use as a second table. You can store the extra table, bring it out when necessary, and butt it up to the regular table for large family occasions.

When you're deciding which table to build, think about where the expanded table will expand to. A table that seats 10 isn't much use if you have nowhere to put it.

Table height

The modern standard for dining table height is 29 in. to 30 in.; however, this has not always been standard. Many historical Shaker trestle tables are 28 in.—or less—in height. (If you're making one to use as a second "expansion" table, as described above, you'll want to make it higher to match your everyday table.) I've made several of these low tables and find them very comfortable. Table height is perceptually interesting. You can notice a difference of $\frac{1}{4}$ in. higher or lower. I've found that tall people are more comfortable sitting at a low table than short people are sitting at a high one (this may be because I'm relatively short). In any case, it's better to err on the low side; never make a dining table more than 30 in. high.

You also need to leave room for the diners' knees—at least 25 in., and 26 in. if possible, between the bottom of the apron and the floor. Trestle tables, which don't have aprons, can be quite low and still have plenty of knee room, but tables with aprons must be higher.

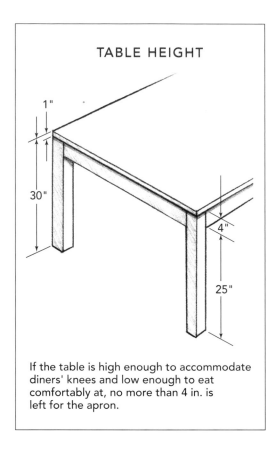

TABLE HEIGHT

If the table is high enough to accommodate diners' knees and low enough to eat comfortably at, no more than 4 in. is left for the apron.

Because of these conflicting requirements, the apron itself can't be very large. Assuming a 1-in.-thick tabletop, applying the 30-in. maximum for table height and the 25-in. minimum for knee room leaves a maximum of only 4 in. for apron height.

Place settings

Before you can decide how large a table to build, you need to know how much room each diner will occupy.

The minimum place setting size for an adult is 24 in. wide by 16 in. deep, with an additional 5 in. of depth for salt-and-pepper shakers, ketchup, candles, and so on. Minimum space is what is allocated for place settings at crowded lunch counters; it doesn't allow for much elbowroom. Minimum place settings can be used for breakfast and kitchen tables and other informal dining.

The optimal place setting is 30 in. wide by 18 in. deep with an additional 9 in. of depth for shared space. The larger space allows for

A MINIMUM DINING TABLE FOR FOUR

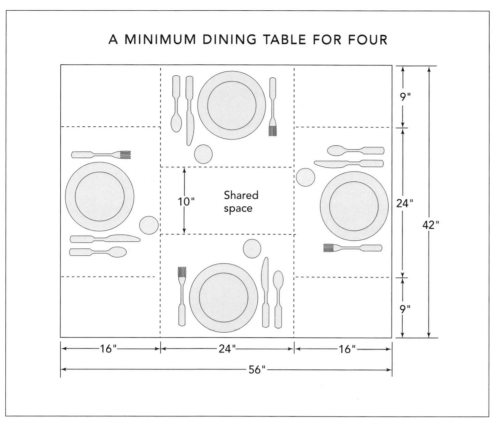

AN OPTIMUM DINING TABLE FOR FOUR

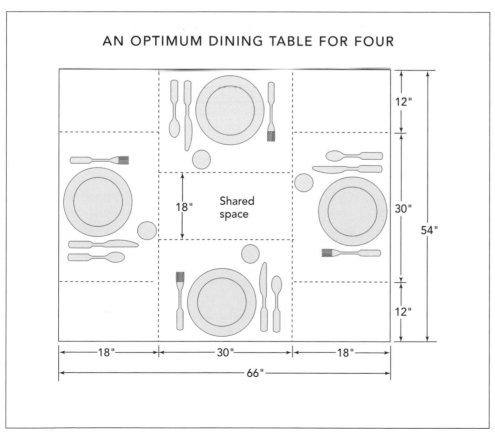

OPTIMUM TABLE SIZES

Rectangular Tables

Place Settings	Minimum Size	Optimum Size
4	42 in. x 56 in.	54 in. x 66 in.
6	42 in. x 80 in.	54 in. x 96 in.
8	42 in. x 104 in.	54 in. x 124 in.
10	42 in. x 128 in.	54 in. x 156 in.
12	42 in. x 152 in.	54 in. x 186 in.

Round Tables

Place Settings	Minimum Diameter	Optimum Diameter
4	48 in.	60 in.
6	60 in.	72 in.
8	72 in.	not recommended

serving dishes, elbowroom, and comfortable adult conversation.

Using the minimum and optimum place settings, you can determine how large a table you need. Combining four minimum place settings results in a minimum four-person dining table size of 56 in. long by 42 in. wide. The shared space in the middle is small—only 24 in. by 10 in. It's hard to serve from a table of this size, but the table is adequate for informal dining.

A dining table for four with optimum place settings measures 66 in. long by 54 in. wide. This table has plenty of space for serving and comfortable dining.

If your room is large enough, design the table to accommodate optimum place settings for the people who will use the table on a regular basis. If you entertain regularly, consider building an expandable table. Remember that a formal dining table for 10 people is 13 ft. long and an informal one almost 11 ft. long. To find out whether you will be able fit an expanded table into your dining area, see "Room Clearance" on the facing page.

Circular tables are also popular. The chart above gives the minimum and optimum table diameters for seating up to eight people. The problem with circular tables is that they waste a lot of space. As the table gets bigger, the shared space in the middle becomes harder to reach. The table ends up taking more and more space in the room while the shared middle is unused. A good compromise is a round table that seats four people comfortably and expands with leaves to become a racetrack-oval table seating a larger number.

Clearance

In theory, a 10-ft. by 10-ft. room could hold a 10-ft. by 10-ft. table. However, you and your family would have to be very thin to sit at the table or walk around it. When you design a table, be sure to leave space for seating and access.

Not everyone has a large enough dining room, so you may need to compromise. I recommend compromising on circulation space first, then on the table size and seating zone. You probably don't need to walk all around the table. You may be able to manage if you leave adequate circulation space on three sides, or two, or even on one side of the table. If you're short on room, don't put a sideboard in the dining area. Serve from the table or from the kitchen. Storing china and silver in the

ROOM CLEARANCE

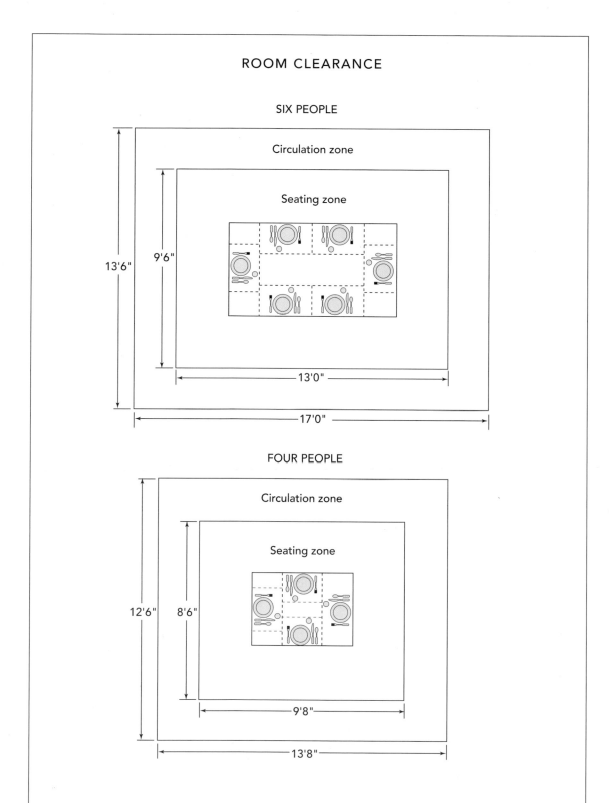

SIX PEOPLE

Circulation zone

Seating zone

13'6"

9'6"

13'0"

17'0"

FOUR PEOPLE

Circulation zone

Seating zone

12'6"

8'6"

9'8"

13'8"

kitchen is more efficient anyway because that's where the food is put into serving dishes and the dishes are washed.

Getting in and out of a chair at the table requires a minimum 30-in. to 36-in. seating zone between the table and the wall or other obstruction. In addition, people walking behind the seated persons need an additional circulation space of 24 in. to 36 in. To calculate how large a table a room can accommodate, measure the room and work backwards.

The bottom illustration on p. 9 shows a table with four minimum place settings, a minimum seating zone of 30 in., and a minimum circulation zone of 24 in. To accommodate minimal seating, the room must be approximately 9 ft. wide by 10 ft. long. To allow circulation on all four sides, the room must be almost 13 ft. wide by 14 ft. long.

The top illustration on p. 9 shows a table for six with optimum place settings. With minimal seating space, the room must be at least 9½ ft. wide by 13 ft. long. Circulation space increases the room size to a minimum of 13½ ft. wide by 17 ft. long.

Sideboards, china cupboards, and other furniture all add to the room size requirements.

TABLE CONSTRUCTION

Three different forces must be considered in designing a table: weight on top of the table, lateral force against its side, and torque on the edge of the tabletop. Seasonal wood movement must also be taken into account.

Weight

The table must be strong enough to support not only dinner but also bags of groceries, the baby in her carrier, and maybe even a person changing a light bulb or two people singing "Alice's Restaurant!" I design my tables to support 400 lb. The trick is to make the top thick enough so it won't split in two and to make the legs thick enough to support the load.

Lateral force

Second, the table must support the lateral force that results when someone leans against it or drags it across the floor. Lateral force tends to make the structure rack. You can prevent racking either by putting a brace between each pair of adjacent legs, as you would on a chair, or by building an apron and adding corner blocks.

Torque

If you put weight on the edge of a table, the table shouldn't tip over. This is more of an issue for pedestal tables than for tables with legs. Solutions include making the pedestal wider, adding legs to the bottom of the pedestal to resist rotation, and increasing the weight of the table.

Wood movement

Because wood is a plant product, it has a cellular structure and contains a high percentage of water. Even after the cells are dead, they can absorb and release moisture, which causes them to expand and contract. As lumber is dried, it loses moisture and shrinks. Kiln-dried hardwoods typically have moisture contents below 10 percent. However, bringing that lumber into a centrally heated house as furniture can cause it to dry out and shrink even further. Damp weather causes the cells to absorb atmospheric moisture and expand. You can slow down this cycle by sealing the wood with a finish, but you can't stop it completely, no matter what you do.

Hydraulic forces are much stronger than any mechanical fastener you can use. Unless you take seasonal wood movement into consideration, tabletops will split in the middle and joints will fail. Depending upon the species of wood used, a board will expand and contract up to 1.5 percent, or 3/16 in. per ft. That doesn't sound like much, but on a 54-in.-wide table it amounts to an expansion/contraction cycle of almost ¾ in.

Much of the finest hardwood is made immediately into veneer.

Luckily, wood movement occurs significantly in only one direction—across the grain. The cell structure keeps cells from expanding and contracting in the direction the grain runs.

Different species of woods expand and contract at different rates. However, you don't have to know exactly how a board will react. It's enough to remember two rules and build accordingly:

1. Wood movement across the grain is significant and must be considered.
2. Wood movement with the grain is insignificant and can for all practical purposes be ignored.

Tabletops

You can choose among four options in constructing a tabletop: a single, wide plank; a glued-up solid-wood top; a veneered top over plywood or medium-density fiberboard (MDF); and a torsion-box top.

First, you could find a single board wide enough to make the top. A single-board, solid-wood top is always dramatic and, with the right plank, can be extraordinarily beautiful, since color and grain will match across the entire width. The disadvantage is that it is almost impossible to keep a single-board tabletop flat, due to seasonal wood movement. Old-growth wood is hard to find and hard to work with because of its size and weight. Making this sort of tabletop demands material-handling equipment beyond the resources of most hobbyists and beyond the scope of this book.

The more practical way to fashion a solid-wood top is to glue up boards edge to edge until they reach the width you need. Solid-wood tops have a certain mystique; I love them myself. They denote quality and permanence, they have character, and they're somehow close to the tree. The joinery used to make tables from solid wood is well tested and very strong. There are also well-accepted methods of repairing this work. This is the easiest way to make an heirloom-quality table and is used in most of the tables in this book.

Sheet stock and veneer

The third way to make a tabletop is to use modern sheet goods such as furniture-grade plywood, particleboard, or MDF. You can use these materials as is, if you buy them pre-veneered, or you can veneer over them yourself. You'll need to add a solid-wood edge to resist the dings of normal wear and tear.

Sheet goods offer many advantages: They are relatively inexpensive and, unlike solid wood, they are dimensionally stable. If properly made, stored, and handled, they arrive flat and stay flat. Using preveneered sheets avoids a lot of work. Simply cut the sheet to size, attach a hardwood edge, cut a profile on the edge, sand, and call it done.

If you veneer your own panels, you can get wonderful results. The invention of the vacuum press has made the production of veneered panels easy and relatively cheap. The choice of available veneers is astounding. Most of the world's best and most beautiful wood is never cut into boards; it's immediately made into veneer.

Sheet goods also have disadvantages, some alleged and others real. The most common

While the table is comfortable for six, seating four people allows for more gracious, formal dining.

objection is that the technology used to make them, while sound from an engineering standpoint, is historically unproven. However, since sheet goods are artificially aged when they are tested, my guess is that this objection doesn't carry much weight.

Another objection is that many sheet goods are made using glues that outgas low levels of formaldehyde for years. However, there are now sheet goods available that are certified to be free of formaldehyde.

Veneer work seems mysterious to the uninitiated. You need special techniques and tools to use it. But when you come down to it, it's pretty simple. Veneer is just wood. You glue it

to a substrate and then sand it as if it were a solid board. The last three projects of this book feature tables whose tops are veneered over sheet goods.

A real drawback of sheet goods is that they don't take mechanical fashioners, such as screws, as well as solid wood. This means that attaching the tabletop to the legs or pedestal will take special care. I don't use screws in MDF unless I can use a lot of them. You can get specially designed screws for particleboard, which make a strong connection provided the screws are long enough. Plywood seems to hold screws as well as solid wood.

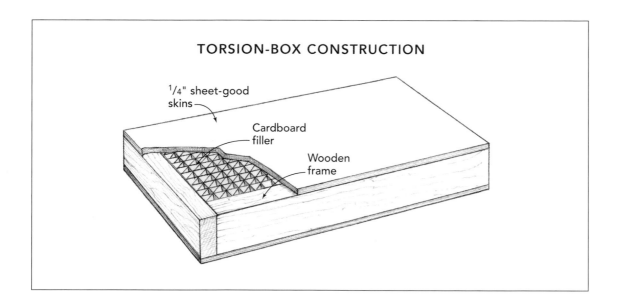

TORSION-BOX CONSTRUCTION

1/4" sheet-good skins

Cardboard filler

Wooden frame

Torsion-box construction

The last way to make a tabletop is to construct a torsion box and veneer over it. Hollow-core doors and airplane wings are good examples of torsion boxes. The advantage of a torsion box is that it is both lightweight and very strong. Although torsion-box construction is typically reserved for large tables like conference tables, it can be a good choice for a dining table larger than the standard 4-ft. by 8-ft. sheet.

The torsion box is constructed by building a wooden frame in the shape of the planned table. One or more 1/4-in. sheets of plywood or MDF are glued to one side of the wooden frame. If multiple sheets are used, they are abutted with their edges resting on an internal wooden frame. The hollow is filled with a corrugated product made for this purpose, and a second sheet (or sheets) of sheet good is glued to the other side of the structure. The entire structure is then placed in a vacuum bag until the glue cures. Once the glue cures, the structure is very strong and can be veneered. The strength of the structure lies in the sum of the gluelines.

Legs and pedestals

Since solid wood resists compression well, table legs are almost always made from solid wood. Even if you veneer over them, it is better to veneer over solid wood than to use MDF,

which just isn't strong enough. Be sure to choose a species of wood appropriate to the style of table you're building. Shaker-style legs made out of zebrawood, for example, look incongruous.

Pedestals, however, can be made of plywood. Modern designs often specify large geometric shapes for pedestals—round, square, rectangular, and others.

A large piece of solid wood would be too heavy to work with and would crack due to seasonal wood movement, while a large plywood pedestal is lighter but still strong enough to support the table. You can veneer over the plywood.

Another option for large pedestals is to make a hollow construction using solid wood. The void in the middle relieves the internal stresses and prevents cracking. This hollow construction can then be turned on a lathe.

The leg assembly

The connection between the legs or pedestal and the tabletop must be strong enough to resist all the downward, lateral, and torque forces. Legs and pedestals cannot be directly attached to a thin top. The top of the leg has a small surface area, and because it's end grain it won't glue well. Also, levering the end of the leg by, say, dragging the table across the floor could rip the leg from the thin tabletop.

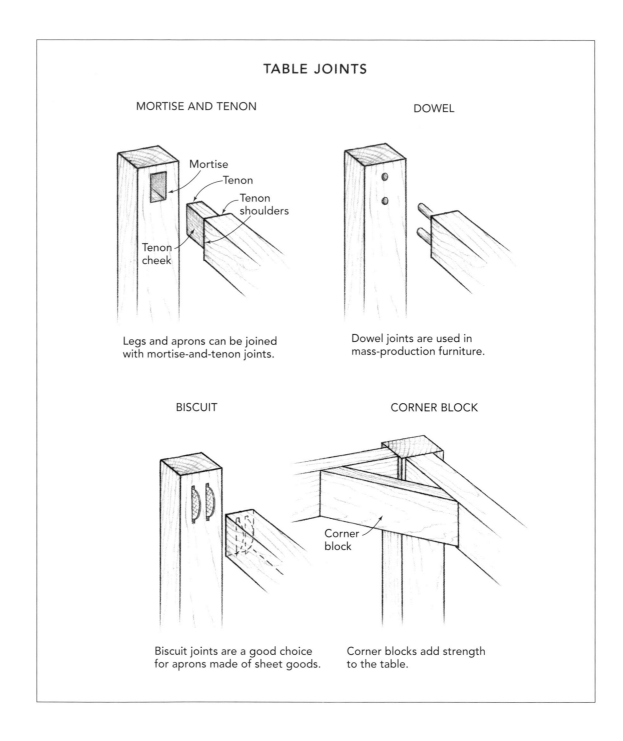

TABLE JOINTS

MORTISE AND TENON

Mortise

Tenon

Tenon
shoulders

Tenon
cheek

Legs and aprons can be joined
with mortise-and-tenon joints.

DOWEL

Dowel joints are used in
mass-production furniture.

BISCUIT

Biscuit joints are a good choice
for aprons made of sheet goods.

CORNER BLOCK

Corner
block

Corner blocks add strength
to the table.

(Needless to say, even a well-constructed table should not be dragged across the floor. Round up enough people to pick the table up and carry it.)

To avoid these problems, legs are typically tied together with aprons and corner blocks or with stretchers before attaching the whole assembly to the tabletop using mechanical connectors.

You can use one of several methods to join the aprons to the legs. Mortise-and-tenon joinery is the traditional mechanism for a joint where the end of one piece of wood (the apron) abuts the side of the other (the leg). It offers a robust mechanical connection, with the tenon extending into the mortise. The shoulders of the tenon keep the joint from racking and hide the insertion point. In addition to the mechanical connection, the tenon's faces offer a large glue surface. This combination makes mortise-and-tenon joinery very strong. Most of the tables in this book use mortise-and-tenon joinery, although other joints such as bridle joints are also used.

You can also use dowels to butt-join two pieces. The resulting joint is nowhere near as strong as the traditional mortise-and-tenon joint, since the mechanical connection is small and there is little glue surface. However, doweling is widely used in production furniture because it is quick and inexpensive, and lends itself to automation.

A good way to join aprons made of plywood, particleboard, or MDF to solid-wood legs is to use biscuits. The biscuit swells when exposed to water-based glue, locking the pieces into place and thus making the joints very strong. Biscuits should be used only with water-based glue from the polyvinyl acetate (PVA) family, such as the familiar yellow and white carpenter's glues. Research has shown that two biscuits are much stronger than a single one, so, if possible, double up at every joint.

Corner blocks brace the corners and help distribute the forces of lateral motion. They are very effective and are used not only in tables but also in chairs and other furniture subject to lateral forces. You can buy metal corner blocks to save time or make them yourself out of hardwood. I think the hardwood blocks are stronger, since they are both glued and screwed in place, while the metal blocks are simply screwed in place.

The pedestal assembly

The easiest way to attach a pedestal to a tabletop is to join it first to a wood or plywood subtop. (Never use particleboard or MDF for subtops; they're not strong enough.) Make a tenon on the top of the pedestal and drill a

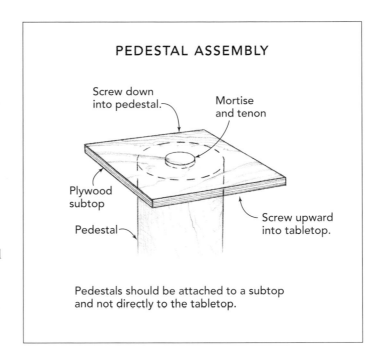

PEDESTAL ASSEMBLY

Screw down into pedestal.

Mortise and tenon

Plywood subtop

Pedestal

Screw upward into tabletop.

Pedestals should be attached to a subtop and not directly to the tabletop.

hole in the subtop for the tenon to fit into, then screw down through the subtop into the pedestal. Finally, screw up through the subtop into the tabletop.

Attaching the tabletop

Normal wood movement must be taken into account when attaching a solid-wood tabletop to its leg assembly or pedestal assembly. Solid wood expands and contracts with the amount of moisture in the air. Without an allowance for wood movement, the top is sure to crack. Special fasteners have been designed to accommodate this wood movement.

The simplest fastener to use is called, appropriately enough, a tabletop fastener. This is a Z-shaped piece of steel running in a ⅛-in. groove in the apron and screwed to the underside of the table. If the fasteners are placed along the width of the tabletop, they will ride in the groove as the top expands and contracts, while still holding the top to the leg assembly. They are very easy and fast to use.

Fasteners hold the tabletop to the apron while allowing for seasonal wood movement.

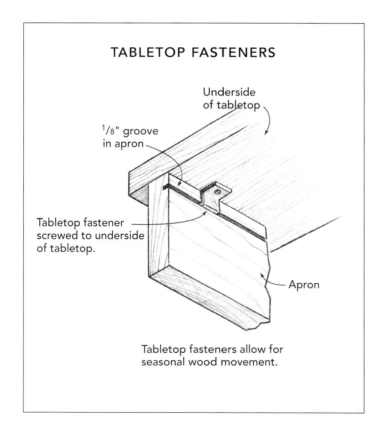

TABLETOP FASTENERS

Underside of tabletop

¹⁄₈" groove in apron

Tabletop fastener screwed to underside of tabletop.

Apron

Tabletop fasteners allow for seasonal wood movement.

You can make your own tabletop fasteners from hard maple. Just make sure the grain runs from side to side, not up and down, or the short grain will break off.

Another common fastener, called a desktop fastener, looks like a figure eight (see the photo above). To use, rout a recess in the top of the apron and screw one-half of the figure eight into the recess. You then screw through the other part of the figure eight up into the underside of the table. As the tabletop expands and contracts, the fastener pivots around the screws.

Fasteners must not be placed on all four sides of the apron but only on the two sides perpendicular to the direction of the grain. They accommodate the expansion/contraction cycle by allowing the fasteners to slip sideways in the grooves.

Attaching a plywood or other sheet-good tabletop to the apron structure is straightforward because sheet goods are stable even when the humidity fluctuates. Typically you attach it using screws—you'll need more of them for MDF or particleboard than you will for plywood. If you want to be absolutely certain, biscuit-join the top to the apron. It's a job, though, to register the biscuit joiner and get everything lined up right.

To attach a pedestal assembly to a tabletop made of MDF, glue a piece of plywood to the underside of the tabletop before screwing the plywood into it. The plywood must be big enough to distribute the torque load and provide a large enough glue surface to hold it in place. One-third to one-half the width of the table is about right.

Other table hardware

Other types of specialized hardware for tables include extension slides that allow tables to expand and hold leaves, sash locks to tie two halves of a table together, and table pins and aligners to align leaves together (see the photo below). These fixtures are available by mail order from most hardware and tool catalogs

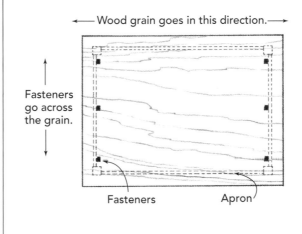

PLACEMENT OF FASTENERS

Fasteners are placed only on the cross-grain aprons of solid-wood tabletops because wood movement is significant only across the grain.

←— Wood grain goes in this direction.—→

Fasteners go across the grain.

Fasteners　　　　Apron

Table expansion hardware, table locks, and alignment pins are available by mail order.

TABLE SHAPES

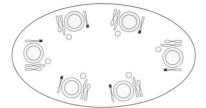

Ellipse

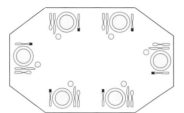

Polygon

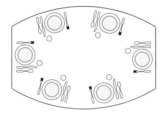

Boat

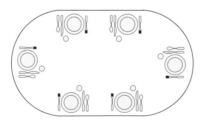

Racetrack oval

(see Sources of Supply on p. 183). I will discuss some of them more extensively in the projects that describe expandable tables.

TABLE SHAPES

To my eye, rectangular tables are the most formal and circular tables the most casual, with other shapes occupying a range between them. Squares, ellipses, and polygons are all popular for dining tables. The racetrack oval shown in the illustration at left is especially popular because it is the result of expanding a circular table with rectangular leaves.

Elliptical and polygonal tables cut off the corners of the rectangle, leaving less serving space on the table. Shown in the illustration at left is the optimum table configuration for six superimposed on tabletops of different shapes. You should either use a pedestal as a base for these shapes, or else think carefully about leg placement so that diners don't end up straddling a leg.

A true elliptical tabletop can be beautiful and dramatic. Its organic shape works well with highly figured lumber or veneer such as flame, quilted, or burl. However, ellipses are difficult to cut accurately and require either making a complicated jig or buying an expensive commercial one. If the top is veneered, edge-banding it is difficult because of the many cauls needed to clamp the banding. Still, something about an ellipse makes it worth all the trouble.

By comparison, polygons are relatively easy to make. They seem modern and sophisticated, and you can make them out of unusual and colorful veneer. One that made a big impression on me was stained with a bright blue aniline dye. It sits right below a giant skylight in a big loft space, mirroring the sky.

MATCHING LUMBER

Much of the challenge of building a solid-wood table lies in choosing the right boards and aligning them so as to unify the piece visually and emotionally. Long after mortise-and-tenon joinery has become easy, you will still be challenged to match color and grain. Beautifully matched lumber transforms a functional table into an unforgettable one.

A century ago, matching lumber was easier because stock was wider and thicker. Today, more boards must be matched and glued together to make up a tabletop or a table leg.

If you have a large bandsaw, a wide jointer and planer, and access to thick and long boards, you can resaw boards using a bandsaw. A whole table made from a single board or even a tabletop made from one board and legs and aprons from another can be perfectly matched for color and grain.

If you can't resaw, choose stock carefully for color and grain likeness. When I go to the lumberyard, I sometimes clean up a patch on the rough lumber using a small handplane to reveal the color and grain (be sure to ask permission before you do this).

Quartersawn vs. flatsawn lumber

In the sawmill, logs are passed through the blade many times to produce parallel boards. The middle, or pith, is discarded. Quartersawn boards with parallel markings running the length of the board are cut from either side of the pith. Flatsawn boards with contour-like markings are taken from the top and bottom of the log (the sides of the board may show different figures). You can tell quartersawn from flatsawn lumber in the rough by looking at the end grain. Quartersawn end grain has a vertical pattern, while flatsawn end grain has a diagonal pattern. Because the pith is discarded, quartersawn boards are typically narrower than flatsawn boards.

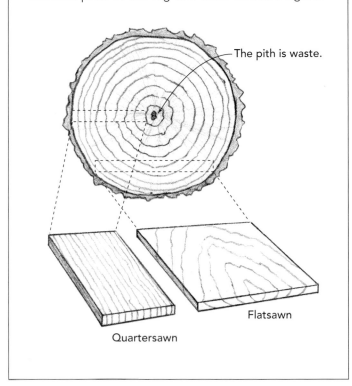

GRAIN ORIENTATION

Quartersawn and flatsawn lumber are taken from different parts of the log and show different figure.

The pith is waste.

Quartersawn

Flatsawn

Don't mix quartersawn with flatsawn lumber on a tabletop; use one or the other exclusively. Quartersawn lumber is easier to match, and, since it's more stable, the tabletop is more likely to stay flat. However, since the boards are narrower, you'll have more of them to mill and glue. Flatsawn lumber is harder to match but a successful match is more dramatic. Since flatsawn boards are wider, there is less milling to do.

In a leg-and-apron assembly, it's better to show quartersawn figure on all four sides of the legs and either all quartersawn or all flatsawn figure on the aprons. To get quartersawn figure all around the legs, you must cut them from flatsawn boards. Legs cut from a quarter-

MATCHING GRAIN

Cut the boards so as to center the figure.

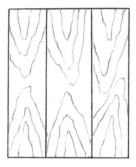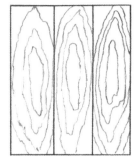

The grain should flow from one board to the next, as in "a" and "c" below.

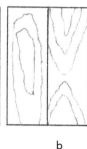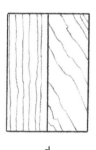

a   b   c   d

sawn board will have quartersawn figure on only two sides. Select a flatsawn board with diagonal end grain to get quartersawn figure on all four sides.

Trestle assemblies look best with uniformly quartersawn figure. However, this is more difficult to accomplish than with legs alone. A reasonable compromise is to show either all quartersawn or all flatsawn figure in each view. For example, you could choose boards that show quartersawn figure on the front and back views and flatsawn on the side views.

Matching the tabletop

To match a tabletop, use the widest boards your equipment can handle, match the boards for the best-looking match, and don't worry about the direction of the tree rings. Some woodworkers believe alternating ring direction will keep the tabletop flat, but I've never found that it makes any difference as long as the lumber is properly milled.

Match adjoining boards so the grain flows without interruption, as shown in "a" and "c" in the illustration above. When the grain pattern stops abruptly, as in "b" and "d," the result is jarring.

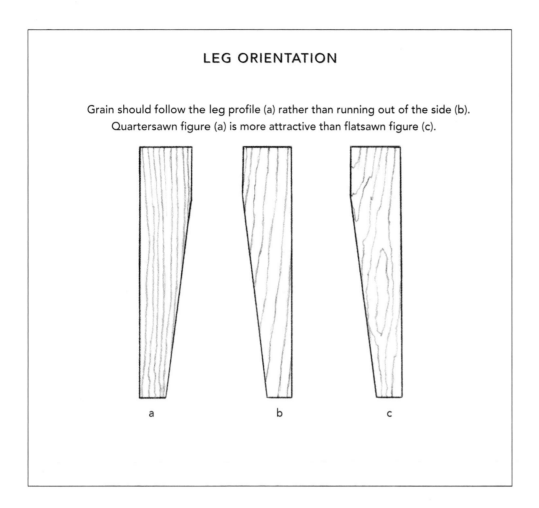

LEG ORIENTATION

Grain should follow the leg profile (a) rather than running out of the side (b).
Quartersawn figure (a) is more attractive than flatsawn figure (c).

a   b   c

You should center prominent figures rather than cut them off. The arrangement shown on the right in the illustration on the facing page is more interesting than the one on the left. You should also match tight grain with tight grain and loose grain with loose grain.

Since heartwood and sapwood are different colors and finish differently, try to choose boards with little or no sapwood. If that's not possible, hide the sapwood by orienting it on the underside of the table. As a last resort, if you're careful you can use it to dramatic effect.

If possible, use the grain to evoke memories of natural beauty: mountains, pools, landscapes. You can do this easily with veneer—that's why people use it—but it is much harder with solid wood. However, when it works in solid wood, the effect is very powerful.

Grain orientation for legs

In table legs, the grain should follow the contours of the wood, as in shown in "a" in the illustration above, rather than run out of the leg, as shown in "b."

For visible crosspieces such as aprons and cleats with flatsawn figure, place the heavier grain toward the bottom because it appears to lift the top.

In all wood matching, all that really matters is the result. Use the rules as a guide but trust your own eye.

Kitchen Table

Many of my childhood memories center around the kitchen table. More than just the scene of family meals, it was the place where my brothers and I did our homework while our mother or our grandmother cooked dinner and where the adults sat to pay bills and drink endless cups of coffee.

This kitchen table, as simple and sturdy as it is elegant, is one where families will want to gather and share the day. In the size shown here, it will comfortably seat four people, and it can easily be scaled to fit six. I've made it in cherry, but maple would work as well if you prefer a lighter color.

This is a good first table project and even a good first woodworking project since it is both basic and challenging. Because it uses the most common type of table construction—four legs, an apron, and a top—it offers an excellent introduction to building with solid wood.

Even if you don't build this kitchen table, you might want to read this chapter. I provide more detail here about basic operations than I will when discussing later projects. The sections on milling rough lumber into dimensioned boards, building a solid-wood top, and mortise-and-tenon joinery are applicable to most of the other tables as well as to this one.

Kitchen Table

THE KITCHEN TABLE offers a good introduction to solid-wood table construction. The four tapered legs join to the apron with mortise-and-tenon joints and are braced with corner blocks for stability. The tabletop, made by gluing up several boards matched for grain and color, attaches to the leg assembly by means of tabletop connectors. The table is sized for informal dining for four adults but an alternate cut list is given for a six-person table.

TOP DIMENSIONS

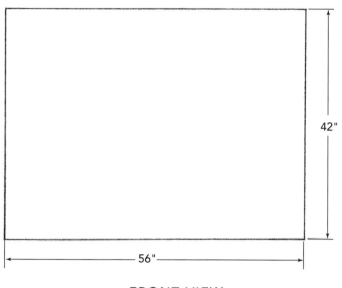

42"

56"

TOP VIEW

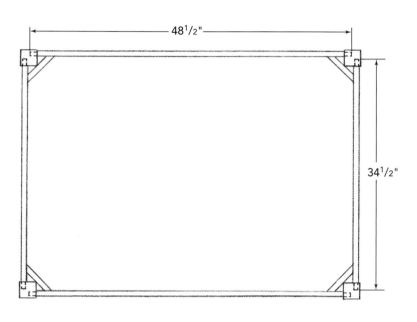

48$^1/_2$"

34$^1/_2$"

FRONT VIEW

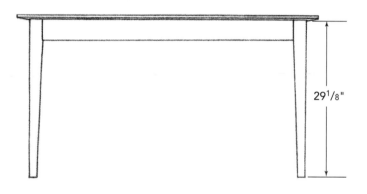

29$^1/_8$"

CORNER DETAIL

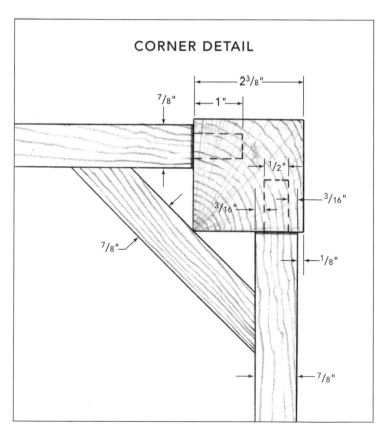

2$^3/_8$"

7/8"

1"

1/2"

3/16"

3/16"

7/8"

1/8"

7/8"

SIDE VIEW

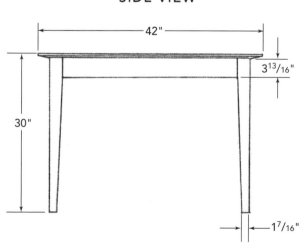

42"

3$^{13}/_{16}$"

30"

1$^7/_{16}$"

BUILDING THE TABLE STEP-BY-STEP

CUT LIST FOR KITCHEN TABLE

Tabletop and Leg Assembly

1	Tabletop	56 in. x 42 in. x ⅞ in.
2	Short aprons	34½ in. x 3¹³⁄₁₆ in. x ⅞ in.
2	Long aprons	48½ in. x 3¹³⁄₁₆ in. x ⅞ in.
4	Corner blocks	6 in. x 3¹³⁄₁₆ in. x ⅞ in.
4	Legs	29⅛ in. x 2⅜ in. x 2⅜ in.

Hardware

8	Tabletop connectors	
16	Steel wood screws	2 in. by #10
8	Steel wood screws	⅝ in. by #10

ALTERNATE CUT LIST FOR KITCHEN TABLE

Tabletop and Leg Assembly

1	Tabletop	80 in. x 42 in. x ⅞ in.
2	Short aprons	34½ in. x 3¹³⁄₁₆ in. x ⅞ in.
2	Long aprons	66½ in. x 3¹³⁄₁₆ in. x ⅞ in.
4	Corner blocks	6 in. x 3¹³⁄₁₆ in. x ⅞ in.
4	Legs	29⅛ in. x 2⅜ in. x 2⅜ in.

Hardware

8	Tabletop connectors	
16	Steel wood screws	2 in. by #10
8	Steel wood screws	⅝ in. by #10

It's best to mill the lumber for all of the parts of this table at the outset. Milling similar pieces (say, the four legs) one after the other saves you setup time and achieves consistent dimensions. After milling, glue up the tabletop and put it aside overnight to give the glue time to cure. Make the legs first, followed by the aprons and corner blocks, and finally complete the tabletop. After you've sanded all the parts, you'll be ready to assemble and finish the piece.

MAKING THE PARTS

Initial sizing

1. Decide which boards you will use for each part, being sure to pick the best boards for your largest, most visible part—the tabletop. You can cut smaller pieces out from around flaws in the wood. The apron board should include the aprons as well as the corner blocks, which are the same width and thickness as the aprons. Using lumber crayon or chalk, mark each board with the name of the part for which it is intended (see "Matching Lumber" on pp. 19–21 for information on selecting boards).

2. Calculate the rough dimensions for each part. Be sure to add at least 1 in. in length and ½ in. in width to the finished dimensions; more is better.

3. Using lumber crayon or chalk, mark divisions on the leg board and on the board for the aprons and corner blocks (see **photo A**).

Milling the lumber

For the table to fit together without gaps at the joints, the boards must be milled so their opposing faces are parallel and their edges meet at right angles. Predimensioned lumber offers little choice of color and grain matching (see appendix 2 on pp. 180–181). Milling your own boards gives you more aesthetic control.

Milling requires, at minimum, a jointer, a planer, and a table saw or radial-arm saw. A bandsaw allows you to resaw thick boards into thinner ones, giving perfect color and grain matches.

Photo A: Mark up the boards for the rough cut.

Photo B: Knock the cutoff against the saw table to determine whether it is solid.

Tip: Use chalk for tentative decisions—it's easier to erase. Lumber crayon is better for final decisions because it won't rub off accidentally.

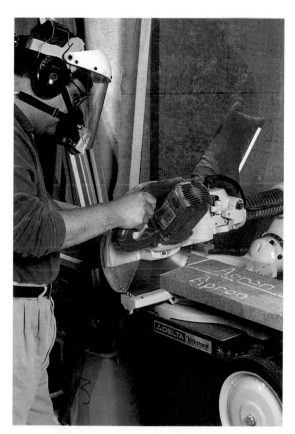

Photo C: Crosscut lumber using a sliding compound miter saw.

Photo D: Before you rip boards using a table saw, you must face-joint them to minimize the risk of kickback.

Tip: If possible, mill the lumber on a dry day. Wood is more stable when the barometric pressure is high.

1. Establish a sound end of each board. Even if the board looks sound, it may have cracks, or checks, which must be cut off. Using a sliding compound miter saw (SCMS) or table saw, cut off the board end 1 in. at a time and knock the resulting cutoff hard against the saw table to see whether it is solid. If it cracks or falls apart, continue cutting off 1-in. pieces until you reach sound wood (see **photo B**). Check for staples in the board—they can damage the brittle carbide of your saw's teeth.

2. Crosscut all of the lumber to rough length using a table saw, radial-arm saw, or SCMS (see **photo C**).

3. Face-joint all of the boards (see **photo D**).

Tip: Tabletop boards don't have to be of exactly equal width. It's more important to choose boards that look right together.

Photo E: Use the same setting to plane all of the boards so that you will achieve a uniform thickness.

4. Edge-joint the boards, holding them against the fence of your jointer. This establishes a square corner between one face and one edge.
5. On a table saw, rip the boards to rough width.
6. Rejoint the face and edges of your boards to mill out the deflections. I sometimes mark the face with chalk so I can see exactly where I am in the process.
7. Finally, plane the parts to establish an opposing parallel face and a finished thickness (see **photo E**). To achieve consistent thickness, put all the boards through at one setting, set the planer to the next setting, and put them all through again. Repeat until you achieve your finished thickness.

Gluing up the tabletop

1. Now that you can see the color and grain, decide how to orient the tabletop boards. Flip the boards, turn them around, and rearrange them until you find a visually striking and organic-looking pattern. If you ripped wide boards to fit on your jointer, be sure to match up pieces that were originally part of the same board. Don't rush this step. Matching grain is one of the most important aspects of working with solid wood.

Tip: Cut two story sticks, one the length and one the width of your finished tabletop. It's easier to use these than to keep measuring the top with a tape measure.

BANDSAW LUMBER TRUING

The order of operations when using a bandsaw is:
1. Edge-joint the parts so you have a flat edge to run against the bandsaw fence.
2. Rip the parts to rough width.
3. Face-joint the parts.
4. Edge-joint the parts again.
5. Plane to thickness.

A bandsaw is preferable to a table saw for ripping boards to width. The bandsaw makes rough dimensioning safer and more efficient. Since there is

no danger of kickback, you don't need to face-joint before ripping to width, as you would on a table saw. Ripping boards releases internal forces, causing them to deflect, so that they must be face-jointed afterwards (this is another reason to leave as much extra width as possible). With a bandsaw, you save a step because you don't have to face-joint before ripping. Even better, you save a problematic step: Face-jointing a wide board wastes material and may leave the edges too thin.

2. Draw a large triangle across the tabletop to help you reassemble the boards later (see photo F).

3. To make sure your clamps are available and ready for use, do a dry practice clamping.

4. Cut a clamp block to protect the wood.

5. Glue up the boards, spreading a thin film of glue on each surface to be glued.

6. Clamp the boards together, alternating the clamps top and bottom to achieve even pressure and keep the boards from bowing (see photo G).

Photo G: When you glue up the tabletop, use clamp blocks to protect the edges, clamp cauls to keep the tabletop even, tape to keep the cauls from sticking, and waxed paper to keep the metal clamps from leaving oxidation marks on the boards.

Photo F: Drawing a triangle across the table-top boards helps you line them up the way you want them.

WHAT GLUE TO USE

For the projects in this book, you need only two kinds of glue: yellow glue, or polyvinyl acetate (PVA) for solid-wood and sheet-good joinery, and urea resin glue for veneer work and lamination. If you want to branch out, try hot hide glue, a good choice for solid-wood joints. I confess to a personal preference for hide glue, but in this book I assume you are using PVA and urea resin glue.

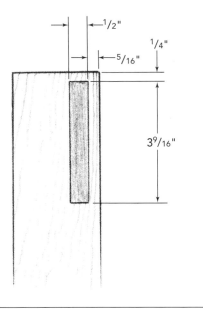

MORTISE MEASUREMENT DETAIL

1/2"

1/4"

5/16"

3⁹/₁₆"

JOINERY AND DETAILS

Making the legs

To construct the legs for this table, lay out and cut the mortises, then cut the tapers. Cutting joinery is easier when the workpieces are square. If you cut the tapers first, you'll have problems cutting the mortises.

Cutting the mortises

1. Start by cutting the legs to final length. Square the end of one leg using your crosscut tool of choice, then set a stop and cut all four legs to the same length. Cut the legs one after the other without changing the stop setting (see "Critical Dimensions" below). It doesn't matter if the legs are 1/16 in. short as long as they're all the same length.

2. Decide which way the grain should run on the legs, and orient the legs so their most

CRITICAL DIMENSIONS

Many woodworkers wonder how precise their measurements need to be. The answer depends on whether you're measuring for a critical or noncritical dimension.

A dimension is critical if a small measurement error will cause the finished piece to function improperly; create extra work for you in building the piece; or make the finished piece "look wrong." The tolerance for critical dimensions should be within a few thousandths of an inch; with noncritical dimensions, you have more slack.

Table leg length is a critical dimension because even the smallest variation will make the table rock. To make the legs equal, set a stop on your saw and cut the legs to length one after the other. Don't take a break and use the saw for something else, or you'll

never get the stop back in the same position and the legs won't match.

The placement of the leg mortise is another example. If it varies, the tenons will have to be individually fit to make the table square—a time-consuming and error-prone operation. To place the mortises consistently, cut them one after the other.

Tools such as tape measures are not accurate enough for critical measurements. Even with high-quality tooling, the human eye doesn't discern gradations of much less than 1/100 in. Critical dimensions should be 10 times more accurate than that. The only way to achieve this level of accuracy is to set up your tooling and mill all the parts that require that dimension at the same time, without changing the setup.

ALTERNATIVES FOR MILLING MORTISES

Although a mortising machine is the fastest way to cut mortises, good alternatives exist. Simplest, cheapest, and most enjoyable is chopping the mortises by hand using a mallet and mortising chisel. First lay out the mortises completely so you'll have lines to chisel to. Be sure to use a mortising chisel, which is thicker than a normal chisel. The thickness acts as a jig to cut square and lever against the wood to remove the waste. With a little practice, this method is very fast.

Another low-tech method is to drill holes using a drill press and clean up using a chisel. I find this method slow and inaccurate, but some people swear by it. With this method you also need to lay out all of the mortises.

You can also use a router, either in a router table with proper fences or with a shopmade jig. This method is very accurate. However, setup time is longer than with a dedicated mortising machine, and the method is more dangerous and error-prone.

Tip: A marking knife makes a finer and more accurate line than a pencil.

attractive faces are outside. Mark the top of each leg with a triangle mark and the inside faces with a witness mark.

3. To lay out the mortises, set a combination square to ¼ in. and use a marking knife to mark the tops of the mortises on the inside and outside of each leg.

4. Reset your combination square to 3⅜₆ in. and mark the bottoms of the mortises.

5. Mark the sides of the mortises on one leg. First set the knives on your marking gauge to the same width as the mortising bit—½ in. in this instance. Then set the fence on the gauge ⁵⁄₁₆ in. away, making sure it is flush against the outside edge of the leg.

6. Position the fence on the mortising machine so the edge of the hollow chisel is on the layout lines. Make sure the chisel is square to the fence. If you don't have a mortising machine, see "Alternatives for Milling Mortises" above.

7. Next, position the leg against the fence and eyeball the starting position of the cut. Cut the mortise, eyeballing the end of the cut (see photo H).

8. Cut the remaining seven mortises. The mortises must be in the same place on every

Photo H: Use the mortising machine to mill the mortises.

Photo I: Orienting the leg taper so that you turn the piece clockwise after the first cut is safer because it leaves more wood on the saw table during the second cut.

leg. Even if you made a mistake in setting up the machinery for the first leg, cut all four legs with the same mistake.

9. Clean up the bottoms of the mortises using a chisel.

Cutting the taper on the legs

The safest way to cut a taper on a leg is by using a bandsaw. Mark the taper line with a pencil, bandsaw $\frac{1}{16}$ in. off the line, and clean up using a jack plane.

If you don't have a bandsaw:

1. Make a jig to cut the tapers (see "Simple Taper Jig" below or use a commercially available taper jig such as the one shown in **photo I**.

2. Using a rip blade on a table saw, cut tapers on the inside faces of the leg. The jig holds the workpiece at an angle while it rides against the fence. Because this method is awkward, it's potentially dangerous. It's hard to hold the workpiece against the jig so it won't slip, and

SIMPLE TAPER JIG

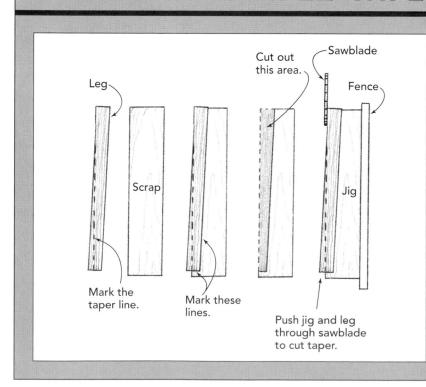

Leg

Cut out this area.

Sawblade

Fence

Scrap

Jig

Mark the taper line.

Mark these lines.

Push jig and leg through sawblade to cut taper.

This jig is so simple that I make a new one each time I need one. Start by marking the taper in pencil on the left side of one leg. Take a piece of scrap wood or sheet stock about 6 in. wide and 2 in. to 3 in. longer than the leg, and lay the leg against it, top facing away from you so the taper follows its left side. With a pencil, trace the right side and bottom of the leg onto the scrap. Following the pencil lines, cut the resulting profile on a bandsaw, cleaning up the edges as necessary. The leg fits into the resulting niche while tapering.

your hand can be too close to the blade for comfort. *Always* use your blade guard and splitter. Orient the leg so you will turn it clockwise to make the second cut. The first taper will face upward as the second cut is being made, leaving a larger surface on the table during the second cut (see **photo I**).

3. Remove the mill marks using a plane, a jointer, or a belt sander.

Laying out the tenons

1. Begin by cutting the apron pieces to length. Square one end of the first short apron piece, then set a stop on your crosscut tool to make the opposing apron piece the same length (apron length is a critical dimension). Repeat for the long apron pieces.

2. Arrange the workpieces in the correct order and draw an orientation triangle on the tops of the pieces.

3. Set your combination square to 1 in. Measuring from the ends of one short apron and one long apron, mark the 1-in. lines.

4. With the marking gauge still set at the width you used to cut the mortises, reset the fence on the gauge to ³⁄₁₆ in. Use the gauge to mark the end grain of one of the short aprons, then reset the combination square to ¼ in. and mark the end grain for the top and bottom of the tenon.

Cutting the shoulders

1. Using a sharp crosscut blade on a table saw, place the marked workpiece beside the table-saw blade and adjust the blade to the same height as the knife mark on the end grain. Measuring from the workpiece is much more accurate than measuring the blade height (see photo J).

2. Using your miter gauge, position a short apron so the knife mark on its top is split by the blade edge (see **photo K**). Set a stop on the miter gauge fence to mark the length of the tenon. If your miter gauge doesn't have a fence, attach a scrap piece and clamp a stop block at the proper position.

3. Unless you have an overarm blade guard and splitter, remove the guard (this is a good reason to buy an aftermarket blade guard).

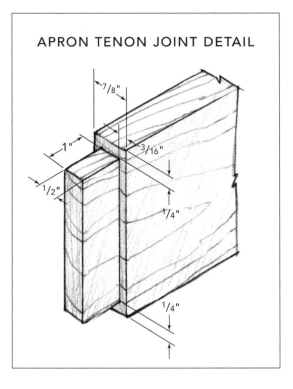

APRON TENON JOINT DETAIL

Tip: If the knife mark is hard to see, rub chalk into it.

Photo J: Adjust the blade height to match the knife mark on the end grain of the apron.

Photo K: The apron piece is positioned so that the edge of the blade meets the mark you made with the knife.

Photo L: Since I have
an overarm blade
guard, I can cut all of
the shoulders with
the blade guard on; a
basket guard would
have to be removed.

Cut the shoulders on all four faces of the board (see **photo L**). If you cut the first tenon too short, adjust the stop and recut. However, if you cut the tenon too long, ignore the mistake. It's only important that the tenons are all the same length.

4. Flip the board and cut the other four shoulders.

5. Cut the eight shoulders on the other short apron.

6. Reset the stop block for the longer aprons and cut the remaining shoulders.

Cutting the faces

Although you can make your own jig, the commercial jig shown in **photo M** is so good and inexpensive that I consider it a mandatory accessory (see Sources of Supply on p. 183).

1. Using a rip blade in your table saw, set up the jig so the first tenon will be a little large, then test-fit the tenon into the mortise until it goes in easily but tightly by hand. Sneak up on the correct width. Remember that changing the jig setting by, say, $\frac{1}{64}$ in. makes the tenon $\frac{1}{32}$ in. smaller, since you are cutting $\frac{1}{64}$ in. from each of two faces.

2. Once the jig is set, cut all of the faces on all of the aprons.

3. Cut the tops and bottoms of the tenons, either by hand or by setting the fence and a stop on the bandsaw. If cut correctly, the mortises and tenons will require no cleanup and will be interchangeable.

Tip: When using a router table, feed the stock from right to left, pushing it into the incoming blade. Feeding stock the opposite way could cost you a finger.

Photo M: I use a commercial tenon jig to cut faces, but a shopmade jig will work as well.

Cutting the beads on the aprons

If you have a router table, make the bead in one pass so there is no chance of ruining it with the second cut. If you don't have a router table, rout the bead by hand, using a bit with a bearing and moving the router left to right.

Cutting the grooves for the tabletop connectors

1. Using a rip blade in your table saw, hold the tabletop connector against the fence and adjust the fence so the blade's right side is just to the left of the connector face. When you screw the connector into the top, the top will be drawn down tight.

2. Cut the groove onto the top of each short apron.

Cutting the corner blocks

Corner blocks help distribute lateral forces across the apron structure. They are very effective: I've seen old chairs and tables with loose joinery that remained usable because the corner blocks were intact.

Corner blocks are simply blocks with 45-degree bevels on each end, glued and screwed into the corners. Although you might think you couldn't glue the block's end grain to the apron's long grain, the 45-degree bevel exposes enough of the long fibers for the glue to hold.

1. Set the SCMS or table-saw blade to 45 degrees and cut off one end of your board.
2. Set a stop at 6 in. It's better to make the block too long than too short—if it's too short, you'll hit the side of the table leg.
3. Flip the board and cut the first corner block. Continue flipping the board until you have four blocks.
4. Drill pilot holes for the screws perpendicular to the face of the corner block. Situate the holes so the screws will enter the apron at the inside edge of the corner block, traveling through the full thickness of the block and as much of the apron as possible.
5. On each end of each block, mark and drill two holes. The screw shank for a #10 screw is $\frac{5}{32}$ in. The holes should be large enough so that the screw shank can slide in and the threads can draw the corner block into the apron (it's worth getting the correct bit). Finally, countersink holes for the screw heads.

Neatness counts here. Identical blocks will be interchangeable when it comes time to screw them to the table.

DIMENSIONING THE TABLETOP

Flattening

1. Remove the tabletop from the clamps and check for flatness using a long level. If the tabletop is within $\frac{1}{8}$ in. or $\frac{1}{16}$ in. of flat, plane or belt-sand off the high points on the top and bottom surfaces (the tabletop won't sit flat unless its bottom surface is flat).
2. If the tabletop is not close to flat, see "Correcting a Badly Cupped Tabletop" below.

Cutting the tabletop

1. Looking at the rough-cut tabletop, decide where to make the final cuts. There may be knots on the ends of the boards, or the clamps may have left a damaged edge. When you've marked a blemish-free area, rip a reference edge along one edge of the panel using your table saw. Place the tabletop right side up so you get a clean cut on the top side.

CORRECTING A BADLY CUPPED TABLETOP

Occasionally a tabletop cups, or warps, after it's glued. A friend of mine made a conference tabletop that cupped so badly that the center of the table was 2 in. below the edges. In this case sanding or planing would result in thin edges or a thin middle. More extreme measures are called for.

The best strategy is to cut the boards apart at the seams, edge-joint them again, and glue up the tabletop again. This should flatten the top enough so that you can plane or belt-sand it to flat. This solution works only if you have enough material to spare: Each cut will subtract more than $\frac{1}{8}$ in. If your tabletop is made from many narrow boards, you can lose a lot of width. Try to leave enough waste so that you can make this correction if you need to.

Photo N: The tabletop panel faces down when you crosscut it using a circular saw and straightedge.

Photo O: If you use a jack plane to cut the bevel, plane the table ends first so any break-out at the end of the cut will be planed off when you bevel the sides.

2. Reset your fence to the width of the table and rip the opposing edge.

3. As the best way to make the crosscut without specialized equipment, use a circular saw and ride it against a straightedge. Note that the top of the panel should face down to get a clean edge on the top (see **photo N**).

COMPLETING THE TABLE

Finishing the edge

This edge treatment, a simple steep undercut, makes the top seem to float above the under-carriage. Interestingly, a thin tabletop doesn't produce the same effect. It takes the full thick-ness of the top combined with the undercut to produce that "floating" feeling.

1. If your table-saw blade tilts to the left and you have headroom, attach a high auxiliary fence to your table-saw fence and cut the bevel using the table saw. Use a featherboard to hold the panel tight and a zero clearance insert to keep it from dropping.

2. Alternatively, use a right-tilting blade if you have enough room to the left of the fence.

3. If you cannot set up the table saw safely, make the edge treatment by hand using a jack plane, as shown in **photo O**. (Even if you cut with the table saw, you'll need to clean up by hand.) Mark the bevel onto the underside and side of the table.

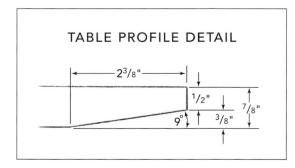

TABLE PROFILE DETAIL

2³⁄₈" ¹⁄₂" ⁷⁄₈" 9° ³⁄₈"

Sanding the tabletop

Many people find sanding dreary, but I disagree—I love to sand. I find the gradual revelation of grain and color beautiful. Sanding gives you a great deal of information about how the finished piece will look. See appendix 1 on pp. 178–179 for general advice about sanding.

1. Starting with the bottom of the tabletop, use a belt sander with a 150-grit belt to remove mill marks, crayon lines, and other marks and to flatten the surface. Keep the belt sander moving! Switch to a random-orbit sander (ROS) with a 180- or 220-grit disk and sand the outside 3 in. to 4 in. of the bottom. You need to sand the outside edge because people will feel under there, but don't sand the center any further.

2. If you're good with the belt sander, use it to sand the bevel. Use a 150-grit belt and then finish with an ROS to 220 grit. If you prefer, use the ROS starting with 80 grit or sand the bevel by hand.

3. Sand the outside edge of the table by hand—a sanding block is easier than a moving machine to hold perpendicular. Start by using a sanding block with 80-grit paper, remove the mill marks, then proceed to the next grit.

4. Turn the tabletop over and belt-sand the top surface with 150 grit to flatten it. Then switch to the ROS and sand to 220 grit.

Sanding the legs and aprons

1. Using the ROS, start with 80 or 100 grit and sand to 220. In machine-sanding, it's easier to reorient the workpiece than to change the paper on the machine. Chalk-mark all of the leg and apron surfaces and

sand them with 80 grit, then chalk-mark the surfaces again and sand to 100 grit. This way if you're interrupted you'll know when you come back that the chalked surfaces still have to be sanded. Continue through the grits. If you prefer, you can sand the leg and apron parts by hand.

2. Sand the insides of the aprons only with the lowest grit to remove construction marks. The tops of the aprons and the tops and bottoms of the legs should not be sanded at all.

3. Next, sand the decorative bead on the aprons by hand. The ROS would flatten the outside edge of the bead and destroy its character.

4. To break the sharp edges and corners, use a sanding block with 220-grit paper and sand each with two or three passes. Softening these edges makes the piece more pleasant to touch without changing its look.

ASSEMBLING AND FINISHING UP

If you're well organized, glue-up and assembly are easy. Have all parts and tools ready and at hand so you don't have to look for anything in the middle of the glue-up.

Practice a dry glue-up before the live run to make sure your clamps are available and pre-set, your clamp cauls are ready and in place, your glue bottle is filled, and your dead-blow hammer, tape measure, and other tools are at hand. You'll also find out whether you have to prepare a special glue-up area. For example, if the floor in your shop isn't flat, you should prepare a flat surface to glue up the leg and apron assembly.

Finally, the dry glue-up will tell you whether you can do the real glue-up in the time available before the glue grabs. For this table, you have about 10 minutes—less in hot weather—to glue up eight mortise-and-tenon joints and clamp and square the table. If your dry glue-up takes longer, either use glue that stays open longer than PVA (such as bottled hide glue), or build in points where you can

stop and gather your wits about you. It's better to find this out during the dry run.

Leg assembly

As I mentioned, it's best to glue up the entire leg and apron structure at once so you can square the whole structure.

1. Glue the shorter aprons to the legs. Using a glue brush, which spreads the glue quickly and easily, spread glue into the two opposing mortises. Since the microclimate in the mortises keeps the glue moist, you have effectively extended your open time.

2. Spread glue onto the tenon faces but not onto the shoulders.

3. Insert the tenons into the mortises, making sure the aprons are oriented correctly.

4. Turn the structure upside down onto a flat surface and knock the bottoms of the legs and the apron next to the legs with a dead-blow hammer. This seats the legs and aprons, making them level.

5. Put clamping cauls in place and clamp between the legs with a single bar clamp. Make sure you hit the spot opposite the middle of the tenon on the outside of the leg so you get even pressure.

6. Measure from the top of one leg to the bottom of the other, then compare that measurement with the opposing measurement. If they're equal, the structure is square. If not, correct the assembly by adjusting the skew of the clamp to press in on the longer of the two measurements.

7. Glue up the opposite apron and legs and square them.

8. Spread glue into the remaining mortises and on the faces of the remaining tenons. Insert the tenons, and level the tops of the aprons with the tops of the legs. Clamp between the legs and check for square on the two long sides.

9. Check for square across the top and correct it, if necessary, by clamping across the long diagonal (see **photo P**).

10. Finally, clean up the glue squeeze-out when it gets rubbery but before it hardens completely.

Installing corner blocks

After the glue dries on the leg assembly—give it a couple of hours to be safe—remove the clamps and install the corner blocks.

1. Make a clamp block with a 45-degree V-groove, fit it outside the corner, and clamp through the corner to hold the corner block in place.

2. Using the predrilled corner block as a jig, drill holes into the aprons using a ⅛-in. drill bit. If the corner blocks are a tad short, knock the inside corners of the legs off with a sharp chisel to fit the blocks snugly into the corners.

3. Spread glue onto the end grain of the corner blocks and onto the apron where the corner blocks abut. Using a 2-in. #10 steel wood screw, screw the corner blocks onto the apron. You don't need to clamp the corner blocks because the screws act as clamps.

Installing tabletop connectors

Now you can attach the top to the legs.

1. Spread a protective blanket over your bench or work surface, then turn the tabletop upside down and put it onto the blanket. Turn the leg structure upside down and put it on the underside of the tabletop. Using a combination gauge, center the leg structure on the tabletop.

2. Insert a tabletop connector into the groove on the apron and mark for the screw holes. You'll need four connectors along the short aprons. Measure ⅜ in. from the tip of a ⅛-in. drill bit, and wrap a piece of masking tape around the drill bit to act as a drill stop. Drill the holes and attach the top.

Checking for flaws

You're not done yet.

1. Taking the tabletop off again, examine every surface and corner. Look for sanding marks that haven't been removed, glue residue that needs cleaning up, and dirt and pencil marks you might have missed. Use a sanding block with 220-grit paper to clean up any errors. I once visited a furniture gallery in New York City to see a $50,000 cabinet made by a famous furniture maker. In the reveal where the leg met the cabinet sides, just at eye level, was a tiny bead of hardened yellow glue. This is your chance not to make that mistake.

2. Put the tabletop back on the table.

3. If you sign your work, now is the time. Construction is done. You're ready for finishing.

Finishing

A kitchen dining table gets a lot of wear and tear. It needs a finish that will look good even after it's taken some abuse. I suggest a combination of tung oil and varnish—you can buy the two already combined. Appendix 1 on pp. 178–179 provides more details on using this type of finish. Don't use stain because cherry is already a beautiful color and darkens with age.

Tip: You can remove glue squeeze-out by washing it off immediately with hot water or by letting it dry fully and removing the hardened glue with a sharp chisel or chisel plane. All these methods work; choose whichever is best suited to your operation.

Trestle Table

Traditionally, trestle tables were knockdown tables, made to be moved in pieces. The Shakers were partial to them because they could carry them easily among their scattered communities. Trestle tables are also useful if your guests are the kind who don't bring their own furniture. These tables can be stored in pieces in the back of a closet and easily reassembled whenever a crowd descends on your household.

This maple table, designed and built by Peter Turner of Portland, Maine, is easy to knock down but much too handsome to be stored out of sight. It's fine for every day if you don't need to seat more than six people on a regular basis. Inspired by an early 17th-century table, it is long and narrow like all traditional trestle tables. Trestles aren't as strong as apron-and-leg assemblies, and if they are made too wide the joints could fail.

You will find this table relatively simple to build—in fact, since the joinery is standard and forgiving, it is nearly as good a choice for a first table project as the kitchen table.

Trestle Table

IN A TRESTLE ASSEMBLY, the stretcher keeps the table from racking while the cleats, or cross braces, distribute load across its width. Keys hold the stretcher securely in place. The cleats are screwed to the table using eight wooden tabletop fasteners that slide in grooves cut into the cleats to permit seasonal wood movement.

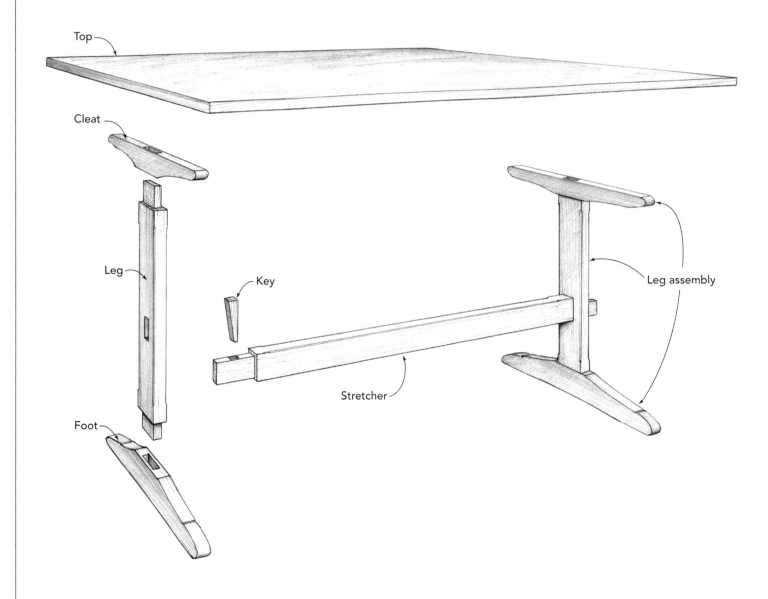

Top

Cleat

Leg

Key

Leg assembly

Foot

Stretcher

TOP VIEW

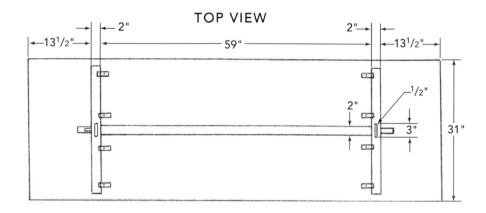

13¹/₂"   2"   59"   2"   13¹/₂"

¹/₂"

2"

3"

31"

SIDE VIEW

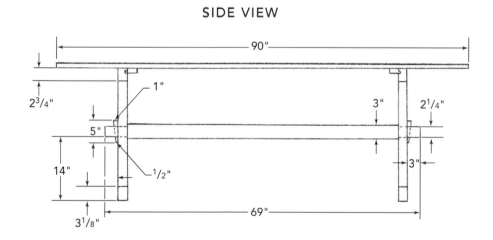

90"

2³/₄"

1"

5"

3"   2¹/₄"

14"

¹/₂"

3"

3¹/₈"   69"

END VIEW

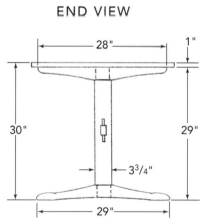

28"   1"

30"   29"

3³/₄"

29"

BUILDING THE TABLE STEP-BY-STEP

CUT LIST FOR TRESTLE TABLE

Tabletop and Trestle Assembly

1	Tabletop	90 in. x 31 in. x 1 in.
1	Stretcher (sometimes called rail)	69 in. x 3 in. x 2 in.
2	Cleats (sometimes called cross braces)	28 in. x 2¾ in. x 2 in.
2	Feet	29 in. x 3⅛ in. x 2 in.
2	Legs	29 in. x 3¾ in. x 2 in.

Connectors

2	Keys	5 in. x 1 in. x ½ in.
8	Tabletop fasteners	2½ in. x 1 in. x ¹⁵⁄₁₆ in.

Hardware

8	Wood screws	#10 x 1½ in.

Peter Turner used curly maple to make this table, but any American hardwood would be suitable. Bird's-eye maple, cherry, curly cherry, walnut, or chestnut would be good choices.

The solid-wood tabletop is like the one on the kitchen table, and the mortise-and-tenon joinery is similar to the joinery used in that table. The only tricky joints are the exposed tenons on the ends of the stretcher and the angled mortises cut into those tenons for the keys.

However, while the kitchen table contained only straight lines, the trestle table has curves on the feet and cleats. The best way to make these curves identical is to use patterns. Patternmaking is a technique that has broad application and will be used in several other projects in this book.

MAKING THE PARTS

Preparing stock

The critical dimensions in this table are the thickness and width of the cleats and feet and the thickness and length of the legs. On the other dimensions, you can be off by a mile and it won't matter.

1. After the wood is jointed, plane all of the tabletop boards at the same time to achieve a consistent thickness. Leave enough extra length in the boards to give yourself plenty of options in matching them.

2. Rip the feet, cleats, legs, and stretcher to rough width on a table saw, then stand these pieces on edge and plane them to width using a planer. Using a planer rather than a table saw to "rip" boards to final width is unusual, but it gives more accurate and consistent results. Thin, wide boards like the tabletop boards would be too unstable to pass through the planer safely. But the other pieces are thick enough to stand on edge, so you shouldn't have any difficulty running them through the planer.

3. Pass all trestle parts through the planer to establish a final 2-in. thickness.

4. Crosscut the cleats, feet, legs, and stretcher to finished length.

5. Don't cut the tabletop fasteners (which connect the cleats to the tabletop and allow for wood movement) or keys to length yet. Simply mill a board about 25 in. long by 1 in. wide by ¹⁵⁄₁₆ in. thick for the fasteners, and one about 14 in. long by a little more than 1 in. wide by a little less than ½ in. thick for the keys.

6. Rip all of the tabletop boards to width on the table saw and joint the sawn edges. Some woodworkers glue up boards with edges directly off the table saw. However, I find I'm

Photo A: It is important to center the mortises on the feet and cleats. Using a piece of scrap the width of the workpieces, mark from both edges, then reset the marking gauge so it splits the resulting lines. Repeat until the lines from the marking gauge overlay when marked from both edges.

less likely to get gaps between boards when they've been edge-jointed.

Building the tabletop

The success of this design, as with all solid-wood tabletops, depends on getting a good grain match. Mix and match your boards to get the best match you can (see "Matching Lumber" on pp. 19–21).

1. Start by cutting clamp blocks and setting up your clamps. Do a dry glue-up to make sure everything is in place. Using PVA glue, spread glue on both edges of the board and glue up the tabletop. Alternate your clamps top and bottom. Place waxed paper between the clamps and the tabletop so the iron in the clamps won't discolor the wood.
2. Leave the top in clamps overnight to allow the glue to cure, then remove the clamps and clean up the glue drips with a scraper.
3. Rip the top to width on the table saw and crosscut the panel to length. If your table saw can't accommodate large panels, use a circular saw run against a straightedge.

Making the joinery

It is always preferable to cut joinery while the workpieces are still square.

1. Mark out and cut the mortises on the cleats and feet, then on the legs (see **photo A**). I use a dedicated mortising machine for these cuts, but you could use a mortising chisel or a plunge router and template as well.
2. Next, mark out and cut the leg tenons using a tenon jig. Either make a jig for this purpose or use a commercially available jig such as the one shown on p. 34.
3. Mark out and cut the stretcher tenons. Since these tenons are 5 in. long and the maximum depth of cut for a 10-in. table-saw blade is only about 3⅛ in, you can't cut them out completely using the tenon jig. The approach I use is to cut a shoulder at the 5-in. length, then cut a second shoulder at the 3-in. length and use the tenon jig to cut out the first 3 in. (see **photo B**). This leaves you 2 in. more to the original shoulder, which you can cut either by using a bandsaw and a fence or by using a table saw and dado set (see **photo C**). In either case, cut the remaining 2 in. a little fat and

Tip: If you're using figured wood, wet the stock before you put it through the planer to reduce chipout and make the fibers more pliable. Wet a rag, squeeze out the excess, dampen the wood, then plane.

Photo B: Leave the tenon a little tight. As an exposed decorative joint, it will be sanded and finished. The sanding will bring it down to the correct dimension so that it slips in and out of the mortise easily.

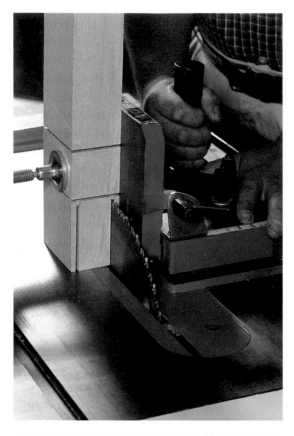

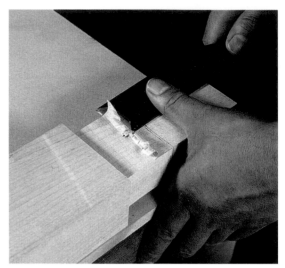

Photo D: Use the 3 in. of the tenon cut with the tenoning jig as a flat surface jigging a sharp chisel. Bring to level the 2 in. of the tenon cut with the dado or bandsaw. Then using a sanding block, hand-sand it to final size.

Photo C: For extra-long tenons, use a bandsaw to reach the area the table saw and tenon jig can't get to. Leave the shoulder a bit heavy and clean it up using a chisel.

then clean up the waste using a sharp chisel and a shoulder plane, jigging the tool against the clean faces cut by the table saw (see photo D).

4. Once you have cut the tenons for the stretcher, cut mortises in them for the keys. These mortises should be slightly recessed into the leg surface so that when the keys are inserted they will maintain tension in the stretcher. To achieve this recessing, mark the inner edge of the mortise at a distance from the shoulder equal to $\frac{1}{16}$ in. less than the thickness of the leg (see the illustration on the facing page). Final sanding will remove about $\frac{1}{32}$ in. from the surfaces, leaving the mortise edge very slightly recessed. Even if you cut these mortises using a mortising machine, cut the angle by hand with a mortising chisel and mallet. Clamp a piece of scrap to the underside of the tenon so the chisel will go through the tenon cleanly. Make sure the wider parts of both mortises face the top of the stretcher.

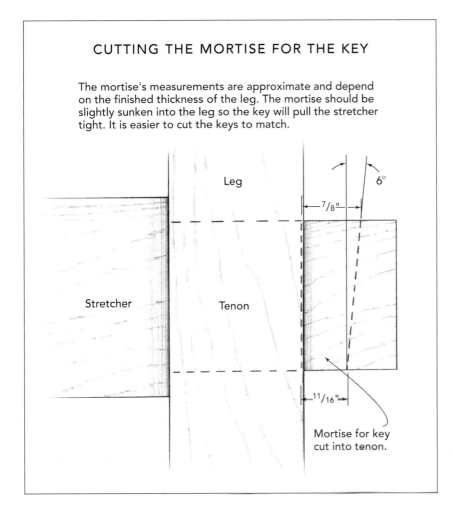

CUTTING THE MORTISE FOR THE KEY

The mortise's measurements are approximate and depend on the finished thickness of the leg. The mortise should be slightly sunken into the leg so the key will pull the stretcher tight. It is easier to cut the keys to match.

Leg

6°

7/8"

Stretcher

Tenon

11/16"

Mortise for key cut into tenon.

Tip: *Tenons that are exposed as decorative joints should be fine-tuned by hand, rather than cut to fit off the machinery like other joints. An exposed tenon must fit easily through its mortise so it can be taken apart, but it can't be too loose. It should be a heavy 1/16 in. less in thickness and width than the tenon you would make for a glue joint. Size the tenon so it's a little too large, then sand, scrape, or plane it down to the correct size.*

Making the cleats and feet

Making the groove for the tabletop fasteners

1. Place a 1/2-in. straight bit into your router and position a fence 1/2 in. away from the bit.
2. Cut grooves in the cleats, stopping and starting the cut approximately 2 in. from the beginning and end of each workpiece.

Making the curved surfaces

To make the curved surfaces of the cleats and feet, transfer the illustration shown on p. 48 onto the workpiece, then cut the parts out.

1. Make a full-sized version of the illustration on p. 48, which shows scaled 1-in. squares overlaying the cleats and feet (the two curves are slightly different, so you'll need to copy both of them). You can enlarge the drawings at a copy shop or scan them into a computer drawing program that can enlarge them. You could also transfer the drawings by hand, marking full-sized 1-in. squares on a piece of paper and matching up where the drawing lines cross the squares. You only have to do half of each drawing because the cleats and feet are symmetrical.

2. To make the curves, trace the full-sized drawings onto the workpieces and use a bandsaw to cut them out. This is the easiest and fastest method since there are only four pieces. If you don't have a bandsaw, you can cut the curves by hand using a coping saw. Clean up the curves with a rasp or spokeshave and sand them smooth. Since these curves are purely decorative and not structural, making exact copies is not critical.

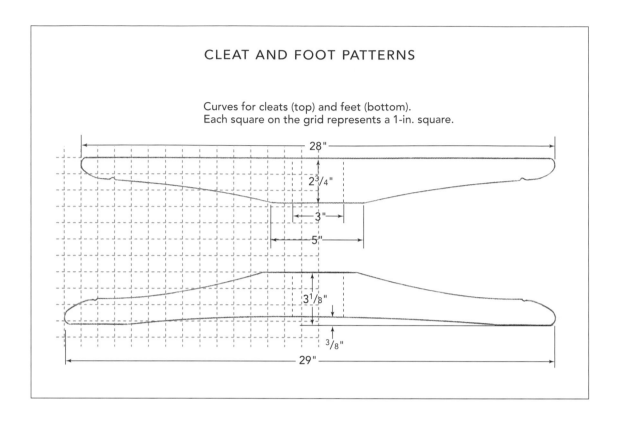

CLEAT AND FOOT PATTERNS

Curves for cleats (top) and feet (bottom).
Each square on the grid represents a 1-in. square.

28"

2³/₄"

3"

5"

3¹/₈"

³/₈"

29"

MODIFYING THE SHAPES OF THE TRESTLE PARTS

Of all the tables in this book, none allows for such easy modification as the trestle table. Because the curves on the cleats and feet are decorative, they can be changed to suit your fancy. Bead details can be changed or removed. The shape of the leg can also be changed, as can the placement of the stretcher—the Shakers preferred to raise it to the top of the leg, where diners' knees wouldn't hit it. The only critical dimensions remain the width of the uncut cleats and feet and the length of the leg. The sum of these three dimensions, plus the thickness of the top, makes up the height of the table. Feel free to experiment with your own designs. The technique for making a trestle table described here remains the same.

The method I used takes longer than simply bandsawing, but it allows you to make any number of identical curved pieces. It requires a bandsaw and a drill press and makes use of a pattern and a cutting tool to follow that pattern (see the sidebar on the facing page). It's a good technique to know and one that's used in one form or another for several projects in this book.

3. Using sprayed contact cement, glue the plan for the foot to a piece of scrap sheet good (I used a ¾-in. piece of MDF).

4. Bandsaw out the waste, leaving just a little over the line of the plan. Don't cut out the bead; just continue the line past it.

5. File, rasp, and sand with a sanding block until you have a perfectly fair curve. Even a little dip in the pattern will show up on the finished part, so take the time to make the pattern exactly as you want the part to look (see **photo E**).

MAKING PATTERNS

Table-saw fences, miter gauges, and even the flat tops of the table saw and router table act as jigs to force the workpiece into a defined configuration with the cutterhead. Normally these jigs force the workpiece into a rectilinear orientation with the cutterhead. But if you want to make identical curved parts or make two halves of a symmetrical curve identical, you must make a curved "fence" that an appropriate cutterhead can follow. This curved fence is called a pattern.

Typically, patterns are made from sheet material. For a pattern that you plan to use many times, ¼-in. or ½-in. clear Plexiglas is an ideal material. Plexiglas mills easily using standard woodworking tools and stands up well to repeated use. If you're going to use the pattern only a few times, almost any material will do. I use whatever piece of scrap I have available, usually MDF or tempered Masonite.

Many tools can be used to follow the pattern. Most common is a router bit with a bearing. In this project, I used a bandsaw with a shopmade guide and a sanding drum with a bearing.

Photo E: Leave the line when cutting out the waste. Then use a sanding block to sand down to the line, fairing the curve as you go.

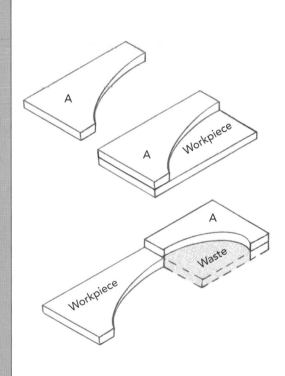

You can duplicate the "A" piece by using it as a pattern to make multiple copies. This is called a full pattern. You can also use "A" to make a work-piece symmetrical by simply turning it upside down. When used in this fashion, "A" is called a half pattern. Making the original pattern is the most time-consuming and difficult part of the dupli-cation process. If you can use a half pattern or even a quarter pattern, you'll work faster and achieve more consistent results.

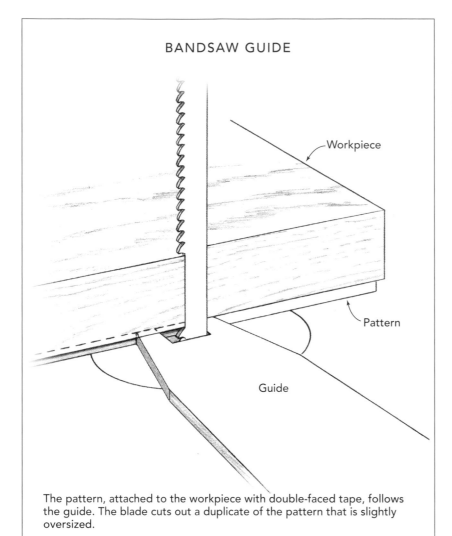

BANDSAW GUIDE

Workpiece

Pattern

Guide

The pattern, attached to the workpiece with double-faced tape, follows the guide. The blade cuts out a duplicate of the pattern that is slightly oversized.

Photo F: The pattern taped to the bottom of the workpiece rubs against the Plexiglas guide, creating identical pieces that can be easily cleaned up using a drum sander.

6. Repeat the process for the cleat pattern.
7. Using double-faced tape, attach the two completed patterns to the workpieces.
8. Set up the pattern-following guide on the bandsaw as shown in the illustration above. Adjust the guide to leave about ¹⁄₃₂ in. of waste—just enough so you can remove the mill marks during cleanup.
9. Use the bandsaw with the pattern-following guide to rough out the first two parts: half of the first foot and half of the first cleat. Don't remove the patterns yet (see **photo F**).
10. To clean up the bandsaw mill marks, mount a drum sander with a bearing onto

the drill press for final shaping. Depending on whether the bearing is on the top or bottom, you may need a secondary table on top of the drill-press table for the drum to fit into. Using a coarse-grit drum, sand the pieces flush with the pattern (see **photo G**).
11. Remove the patterns, flip them, and reattach them to the other halves of the work-pieces. Repeat the bandsaw pattern-cutting and sanding-drum work to complete the first foot and first cleat. To make the second foot and second cleat, repeat the entire process.

Tip: Be especially careful when sanding end grain with the Robo-sander—it's possible to get a kickback in this area.

MAKING THE BEADING DETAILS

The beading detail on the stretcher and legs is made using a ¼-in. corebox bit and a V-groove jig.

Making the jig

1. Tilt the table-saw blade at a 45-degree angle, then put a rip blade onto the saw and make the first cut to full depth.

2. Flip the board and lower the blade so a sliver of material will be left after you make the second cut (see **photo H**). This prevents the cutoff from kicking back. Make the second cut and break off the V-shaped piece of waste, then clean up the groove with a chisel.

3. In the middle of the jig, drill a hole slightly bigger than ¼ in.—the exact size doesn't matter.

Photo H: To make the V-groove jig, set the table-saw blade to 45 degrees, cut all the way through the board, then glue both halves to a thin substrate.

Photo I: Using masking tape, mark start and stop lines on the V-groove block using a combination square. You can start and stop when the lines align with the shoulder.

Workpiece

V-groove block   1/4" corebox bit

Cutting the beads

1. With a 1/4-in. corebox bit in the router on the router table, center the bit in the hole of the V-groove jig and clamp the jig to the router table. Raise the bit to the proper height, and make a few test cuts in scrap wood until you get the results you want.

2. Cut the beads in the stretcher and legs (see **photo I**). To achieve consistent results, make each bead in one pass. Be careful not to burn the treatment at the end of the cut.

3. To make the bead detail on the feet and cleats, clamp a straightedge to each piece and rout the bead. Again, make each bead in one pass.

KEYS AND FASTENERS

Making the tabletop fasteners

1. On your table saw, install a dado set that will plow a 3/8-in. dado, and raise the dado set to 13/32 in.

2. Using a miter gauge, cut dadoes into the tabletop fastener board at 18 in., 12¾ in., 7½ in., and 2¼ in.

3. Change the blade in the table saw to a crosscut blade, and set a stop on your miter gauge fence for 2½ in. Cut off eight 2½-in. tabletop fasteners.

4. Drill a screw hole on the top of each fastener.

Making the keys

Because you cut the mortises for the keys by hand, you should also cut the keys by hand and fit them individually. The blank you milled for the keys should be slightly narrower than ½ in. so the keys can be inserted and removed easily. Keep the blank a little wide until you fit the keys.

1. Cut the keys long (about 7 in.).

2. Using a bevel gauge, measure the angle in the first mortise. Transfer that angle to the workpiece.

3. Cut out the waste using a bandsaw. Using a block plane, trim and clean up the angle.

4. Test-fit the key into the mortise. When the fit is correct, measure 1 in. from the top and bottom of the tenon onto the key. Cut the key to length at those two points.

5. Repeat for the second key.

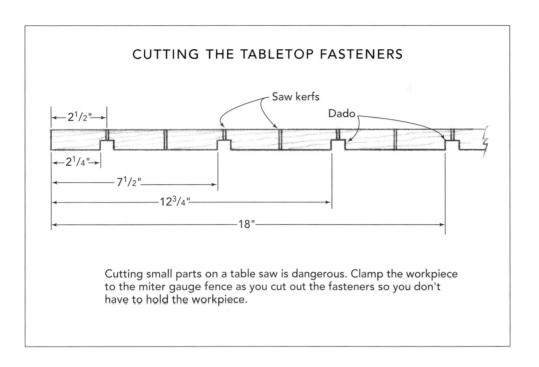

CUTTING THE TABLETOP FASTENERS

Saw kerfs

Dado

2¹/₂"

2¹/₄"

7¹/₂"

12³/₄"

18"

Cutting small parts on a table saw is dangerous. Clamp the workpiece to the miter gauge fence as you cut out the fasteners so you don't have to hold the workpiece.

ASSEMBLING AND FINISHING UP

Assembling the leg structures

In most projects, you would sand all of the pieces before assembling them. On this table, however, if a mortise on a foot or cleat is not perfectly centered, the sides of the legs won't be level with the foot and cleat. You want to sand the pieces to level *after* the joints are together so you can see where the discrepancies are.

1. Assemble both leg structures dry to make sure everything fits together properly. Use waxed paper between the leg and glue blocks, as shown in **photo J**, so the blocks don't stick to the leg. Dry-clamp the assembly to make sure you have everything in order.
2. Spread PVA glue into the cleat and foot mortises on one leg structure and then onto the tenons on the leg. Insert the tenons and

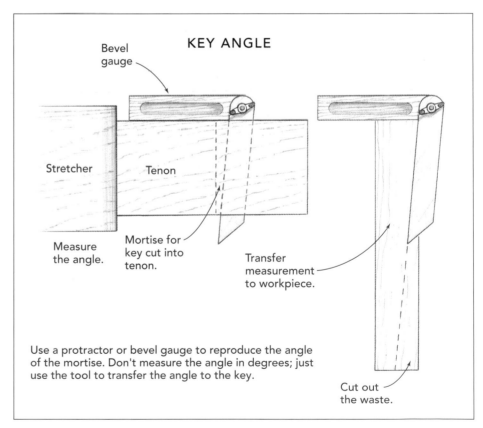

KEY ANGLE

Bevel gauge

Stretcher

Tenon

Measure the angle.

Mortise for key cut into tenon.

Transfer measurement to workpiece.

Cut out the waste.

Use a protractor or bevel gauge to reproduce the angle of the mortise. Don't measure the angle in degrees; just use the tool to transfer the angle to the key.

Photo J: Measuring across the diagonals ensures a square trestle. When the two diagonals are equal, the leg structures will be square.

knock them home with a dead-blow hammer. Clamp the structure, making sure all of the joints are tight. Repeat for the other leg structure.

3. Measure for square across the diagonals and correct any deviation.

Sanding

1. Using a plane or belt sander, flatten the bottom of the tabletop. If you use a belt sander, start with a coarse enough grit to remove material quickly. When the underside is flat, flip the tabletop and flatten the top. Change belts to 150 grit and sand both the top and the

Photo K: Having a variety of shopmade and commercial sanding blocks in different shapes and sizes is useful when hand-sanding.

bottom. Then, using a random-orbit sander, run through the grits, sanding the top to 220.
2. Sand the sides of the table by hand. Using a sanding block, start with 80 grit to remove the mill marks. Run through the grits to 220 grit.
3. With a 220-grit sanding block, break all of the edges of the tabletop.
4. Using a random-orbit sander, start with 80-grit paper to remove the mill marks on the flat faces of the legs and stretcher. Run through the grits to 220 grit. Don't sand the tops or bottoms of the feet or cleats; this would alter the heights of the leg structures.
5. To sand the cleat and foot curves, use a curved, hard rubber sanding tool and sand by hand. Once again, start with 80 grit to remove the mill marks and run through the grits to 220 grit. If you're using a hand-rubbed finish, wet the surfaces after sanding at 220 grit, let them dry, and sand at 320 grit. Don't use the sanding drum without the pattern and bearing to sand these curves—you'll sand dips into the curve. Also, never hand-sand without a tool. You can't level the surfaces properly if you're holding the sandpaper in your bare hand (see **photo K**).

Final assembly

1. Lay a blanket on your workbench, then turn the tabletop upside down on it.
2. Assemble the trestle structure, knocking the keys into place with a light tap from a dead-blow hammer.
3. Turn the trestle upside down and center it on the tabletop. Put the tabletop fasteners in place, and use an awl through the screw holes to mark the screw placement.
4. Remove the tabletop fasteners and drill the screw holes, using a piece of masking tape on the drill bit as a depth gauge. Don't drill through the tabletop! Replace the fasteners and screw them in place.

Final check

Turn the table right side up and, with a sanding block in one hand, inspect every surface with your hand and eye. Remove any glue beads, mill marks, or other blemishes you may have missed. Sign your work if you want to.

Finishing

Peter Turner originally finished this table with wiping varnish. See appendix 1 on pp. 178–179 for application instructions.

VINEYARD TABLE

The vineyard table is almost as old a design as the trestle table, dating back 300 years or more. Some sources claim these tables were used by grape pickers in French vineyards for working lunches, while others say they were used in wineries for wine tastings. Both stories may be true, since the tables fold easily for storage and transportation. The central "harp" spins around on one set of dowels and the tabletop flips on a second set of dowels to create a remarkably compact package.

Neal White of San Jose, California, designed and built this table as a second table for family gatherings at his house. He found it too useful to stow away between occasions, and it's taken up permanent residence in his living room.

The vineyard table is similar to the trestle table on p. 40 except that hinges have replaced the joints between the legs and cleats, and the tabletop is held level by a beautiful harp-shaped support.

I love the look of the figured white oak in this table, but the original tables were made by carpenters from whatever woods were available locally.

Like all trestle tables, this one is easily modified to suit the builder's taste and talents. Vineyard tabletops are typically round or elliptical, but you can make the top for this table in almost any size or shape as long as the width clears the feet when the table is flipped.

Vineyard Table

THE VINEYARD TABLE is similar to a trestle table in construction, except that the cleats are hinged instead of joined to the legs, allowing the tabletop to flip down or be removed for storage and transportation. The harp-shaped structure pivots outward to support the tabletop when the tabletop is set up for use.

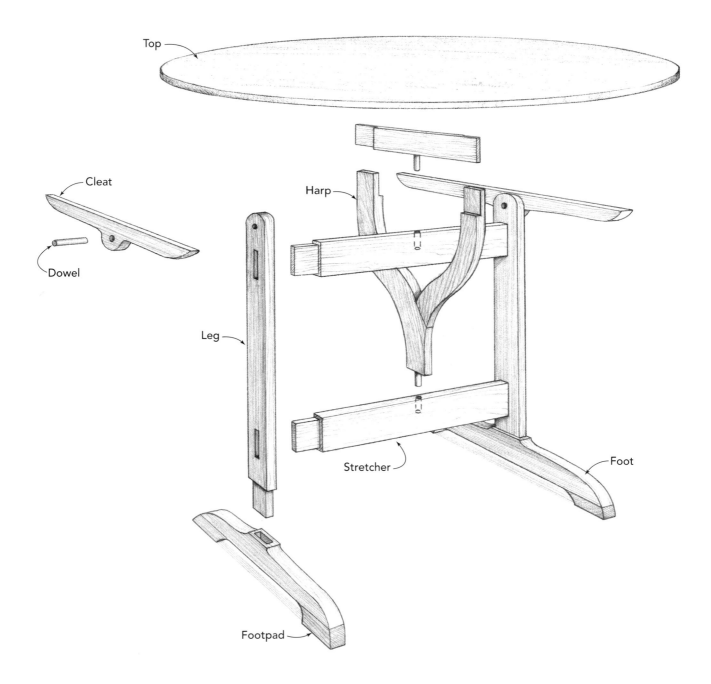

Top

Cleat

Dowel

Harp

Leg

Stretcher

Foot

Footpad

END VIEW

SIDE VIEW

32"

16"

1 7/8"

1 1/2"

3 3/16"

3/4" dia.

R 1 3/8"

3 1/2"

3/4" dia.

3 3/16"

2"

27"

1/2"

2"

4 7/16"

2 3/4"

1"

2 3/4"

3 3/4"

25"

1"

1"

2 1/2"

2"

27"

1 1/4"

22 1/2"

2 1/2"

2 3/4"

1"

1 1/2"

1/2"

HARP

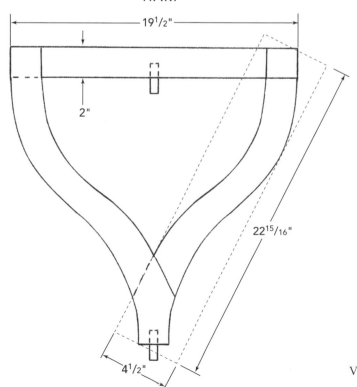

19 1/2"

2"

22 15/16"

4 1/2"

BUILDING THE TABLE STEP-BY-STEP

CUT LIST FOR VINEYARD TABLE

Tabletop and Leg Assembly

1	Tabletop	60 in. x 46 in. x 1 in.
2	Legs	27 in. x 3½ in. x 1 in.
2	Feet	25 in. x 2¾ in. x 1½ in.
4	Footpads[1]	5 in. x 1 in. x 1½ in.
2	Stretchers	22½ in. x 2½ in. x 1 in.
2	Cleats	32 in. x 3³⁄₁₆ in. x 1 in.
2	Harp legs	22¹⁵⁄₁₆ in. x 4½ in. x 1 in.
1	Harp cross bar	19½ in. x 2 in. x 1 in.
2	Leveling blocks[1]	5 in. x 1⅜ in. x 2 in.

Hardware

2	Hardwood wooden dowels[2]	¾ in. diameter x 3 in.
2	Hardwood wooden dowels[2]	½ in. diameter x 3 in.
4	Steel wood screws	1½ in. by #10

[1]The leveling blocks and footpads can be cut from the foot cutoffs.
[2]See Sources of Supply on p. 183.

The elaborate pattern-cutting techniques described for other projects in this book can be used for this table. However, since vineyard tables are traditionally simple, carpenter-made furniture, I've chosen to stick to basic tools and techniques. A jigsaw, coping saw, or bandsaw is all you need to cut out the parts; scrapers, planes, and sandpaper can be used to sculpt them to final shape.

Mortise-and-tenon joints hold the legs and stretchers together, but the lap joint, a very basic joint, is used for the harp pieces, and doweled hinges are used for the moving parts. Another new but simple technique introduced here is drawing the ellipse for the tabletop.

The most challenging task is to fit the pieces together so that the tabletop opens and closes easily and remains level when open. Since every table is slightly different, adjustments to the dowels and leveling blocks should be made dynamically.

MAKING THE PARTS

Preparing the stock

The critical dimensions in this table are the lengths of the legs, the widths of the feet, and the lengths of the stretchers. If these aren't equal, the trestle won't be square. In addition, the width of the tabletop must clear the feet when the table is flipped up for storage. The shape of the tabletop determines how much clearance you have. Rectangular tables have about 45 in. of clearance, while round tables have nearly 49 in. because the curved shape clears the feet.

1. Begin with 8/4 rough stock for the feet and footpads and 6/4 rough stock for all other parts. Although 5/4 might work, you would risk not being able to get all the parts out.
2. Crosscut the trestle parts 2 in. oversize in length. Face-joint and edge-joint the boards and plane them to finished 1-in. thickness, then rip the parts to finished width.
3. Cut all tabletop boards to the same length. When cutting to rough length, leave them several inches oversize. Face-joint and edge the boards, then rip them to width and plane to finished thickness.

Making the tabletop

1. Glue up boards for the tabletop in a rectangular shape, arranging and aligning the boards to get the best match for color and grain. Clamp the tabletop, using plenty of clamps (see the sidebar on the facing page), and allow the glue to cure overnight.

HOW MANY CLAMPS?

The object of clamping is to put pressure on all of the surfaces being glued. Imagine clamp pressure as radiating 45 degrees on either side from the point of application. If the clamps are spaced too far apart, as shown in illustration "a" below, there may be little or no pressure at some points on the glueline. Moving the outer clamps toward the center, as shown in "b," solves the problem in the middle but creates new low-pressure areas near the edges. Some

woodworkers recommend springing the boards so they meet at the ends but gap slightly in the center. The board acts as a combination spring and caul, closing the gaps. I prefer using enough clamps to provide pressure at all points on the gluelines, as shown in "c." In this example, I needed five clamps to get enough pressure. With a panel the same size and narrower boards, I would have needed even more clamps.

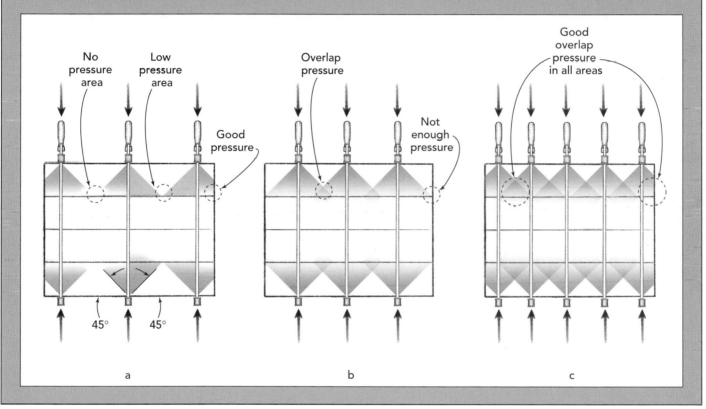

2. After the glue cures, remove the clamps and place the tabletop upside down on your workbench.

3. Draw an ellipse on the underside of the tabletop as described in the sidebar on p. 62, and cut out the ellipse using a jigsaw or coping saw.

4. Finish shaping the ellipse with a belt sander held against the edge or a sanding block with 80-grit sandpaper.

Making the feet

1. Cut the feet to final length.

2. Mark out the ½-in. mortises with a mortising gauge, making sure the mortise is centered on the foot, and cut them out with a mortising machine or chisel.

3. Glue the footpads to the feet and allow the glue to cure overnight (see **photo A**).

DRAWING AN ELLIPSE

Every ellipse has two foci, or focus points. The sum of the distances to the two foci is equal from any point on the ellipse. Following this definition, you can lay out an ellipse with two nails, a pencil, and a piece of string. By varying the position of the nails and the length of the string, you can generate an infinite number of ellipses.

To generate the ellipse for this table, draw a 38½-in. line on the underside of the tabletop, centered along the long axis.

Place a small finishing nail at each end of the line to mark the foci. Next, draw a line crossing the center of the first line at right angles. Mark a point 23 in. along this line—this will be the end of the table's short axis. Take a piece of string about 100 in. long, tie it in a loop, and put the loop around the nails. Adjust the position of the knot so that a pencil held against the taut string will hit the point you've marked. (The loop of string, once adjusted, should measure 98½ in.) Finally, draw the ellipse.

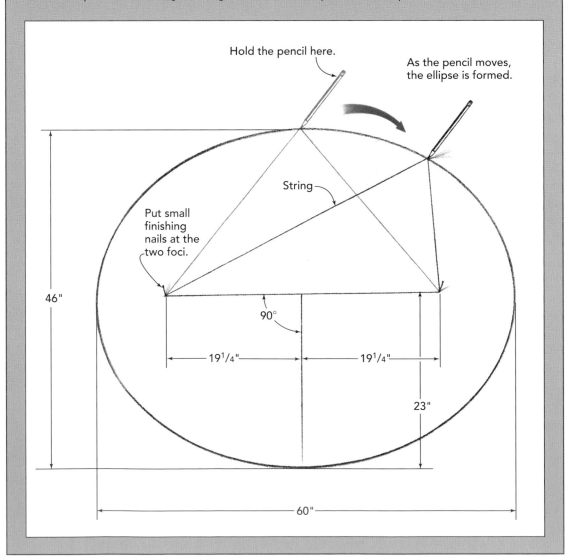

Hold the pencil here.

As the pencil moves, the ellipse is formed.

String

Put small finishing nails at the two foci.

46"

90°

19¹/4"   19¹/4"

23"

60"

4. Enlarge the illustration below to full size or create a pattern of your own, then trace it onto the feet.

5. Using a bandsaw or coping saw, cut out the feet, then plane, scrape, or sand the edges smooth.

Making the legs

1. Cut both legs to final length.

2. Mark out the mortises for the top and bottom stretchers, then cut these with a mortising machine or mortising chisel.

3. At the top of each leg, lay out a 3½-in. square. Draw diagonals between the corners to find the center of the square. Use a compass to draw a half-circle at the top of each leg (see **photo B**).

4. Mark the shoulders of the bottom tenons and use a table saw to establish the shoulder line.

5. Using a tenon jig and the table saw, remove the tenon cheeks. Sneak up on the final width so the tenons will fit snugly into the mortises of the feet without binding.

Photo A: Clamp across the joints to register the sides of the footpads with the sides of the feet.

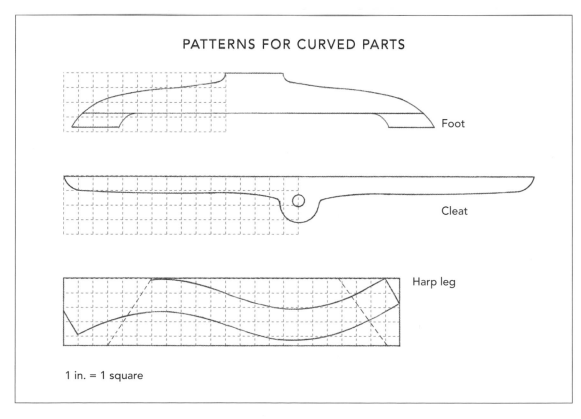

PATTERNS FOR CURVED PARTS

Foot

Cleat

Harp leg

1 in. = 1 square

Photo B: Mark the outside circle before drilling the pivot hole.

Photo C: Forstner bits leave clean entry holes even in difficult wood. Back up the exit hole with a piece of scrap so the exit is clean.

6. Use a bandsaw or coping saw to cut out the half-circle.

7. Sand the half-circle to shape using a sanding block with 80-grit paper.

8. Drill out a ¾-in. dowel hole at the marked center, using a Forstner bit as shown in **photo C** (see Sources of Supply on p. 183). Don't use a paddle or high-speed bit for this hole—you won't get clean or accurate results.

Making the stretchers

1. Cut the two stretchers to length.

2. Find the center of the top edge for both stretchers, then drill ½-in. holes 1 in. deep at both spots to accept the pivot dowels on the harp.

3. Mark the shoulders on one end of a stretcher. Set a stop on your miter gauge, and cut the shoulders for all four tenons on your table saw.

4. Using a tenon jig, cut the tenons. The tenons should fit snugly into the leg mortises. You don't want a loose fit here, so sneak up on the fit until it's just right.

USING A MORTISING CHISEL

A mortising chisel is thicker than an ordinary chisel; the extra thickness allows the chisel to self-jig once the mortise is started. It also absorbs the stresses of mortising. You can order the chisels, and the wooden mallet used with them, by mail from specialty tool catalogs (see Sources of Supply on p. 183).

Body positioning is the trick to successful use of a mortising chisel. Just as you tune woodworking machinery, you must also train your body to use hand tools.

Start by laying out the mortise with a marking gauge, combination square, and marking knife. The knife lines are important because they delineate the top and bottom of the mortise. Clamp the workpiece to your bench so that it's on your right side if you're right-handed or on your left side if you're left-handed. Position the chisel at the far end of the mortise with the bevel facing you, and hold it with your nondominant hand. Align your body with the workpiece (see the top photo). If you do this correctly, the chisel will be vertical.

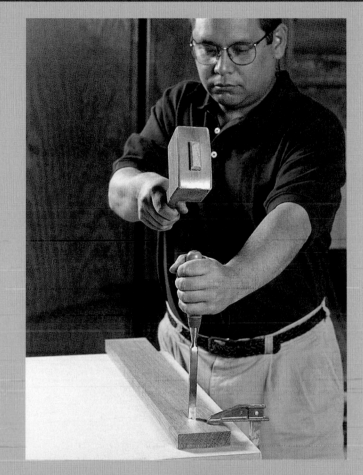

Holding the wooden mallet in your dominant hand, hit the chisel hard with a single whack. Don't be shy and tap-tap-tap on the chisel. The chisel should cut ⅛ in. or more into the wood with each blow. Next, reposition the chisel ⅛ in. closer to you and whack it again.

Pry the chisel toward you, and the chip between the first and second cut will come out (see the bottom photo). Keep working down the mortise until you get to the near end.

Reverse the chisel so the bevel faces away from you, then cut the other shoulder of the mortise square. Now reverse the chisel to its original position and go back to the far end of the mortise. Continue the mortising operation until the mortise is deep enough. The width of the chisel acts to jig the tool in the mortise that's already cut. If you position your body correctly, and you aren't shy about whacking the chisel, hand-mortising can be very fast and accurate.

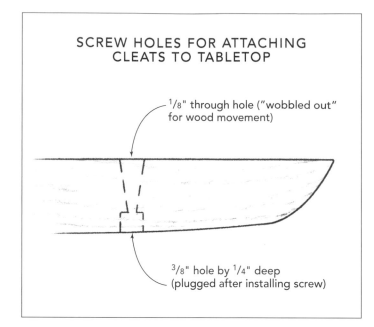

SCREW HOLES FOR ATTACHING CLEATS TO TABLETOP

$^1/8$" through hole ("wobbled out" for wood movement)

$^3/8$" hole by $^1/4$" deep (plugged after installing screw)

Photo D: If you cut your own plugs, you can match the grain direction and make the plugs almost invisible. Clamp the stock to the drill-press table so the workpiece doesn't spin.

Tip: For the harp legs, the two lap joints are on the same side. The two halves of the harp are identical.

Making the cleats

1. Mark the positions for the pivot holes.
2. Mark the positions for the 1⅜-in. radius circles.
3. Either enlarge the illustration on p. 63 to full size or make up your own shape, then mark the pattern onto the cleats.
4. With a ¾-in. Forstner bit, drill out the pivot holes.
5. Saw out the pattern using a bandsaw or coping saw, getting as close as you dare to the line. Mill up to your lines using planes, scrapers, and sanding blocks with 80-grit sandpaper.
6. Mark for and drill the four tabletop attachment screw holes on the cleat bottoms. First drill the plug recesses ⅜ in. in diameter by ¼ in. deep and 3 in. from each cleat end. Through the center of each recess, drill a hole ⅛ in. in diameter all the way through the cleat, "wobbling out" the bottom slightly to allow for seasonal wood movement (see the illustration above).
7. Using a ⅜-in. plug cutter as shown in **photo D**, make four plugs from scrap.

Making the harp

The harp is assembled with lap joints that are glued but not screwed or pinned together. Cutting them can be complicated because they are angled, but if you follow the sequence you won't have any trouble. As always, cut the joinery while the workpieces are still square, then cut out the shapes.

1. Practice this joint on scrap wood first. Put a dado set on your table saw, and using two pieces of scrap the same thickness as the harp pieces, mark half the width on each of them. Raise the dado set so it just meets the half-width line, and make two cuts in the scrap using a miter gauge (see **photo E**). Test the joint, adjusting the height of the dado set until you achieve a perfect fit. Adjusting height dynamically is much more accurate than trying to measure. Now that the scrap joint fits, you're ready to cut your money joints.
2. Cut the two harp legs to length.
3. Rotate your miter gauge counterclockwise, setting it to a heavy 61 degrees. Set a stop block on the miter gauge, and cut the shoulder of the lap joint for the top joint on one leg. Repeat the process for the second leg, then

Photo E: Cut the joint slightly thick, then turn the practice piece over to see the difference between the blade and the remaining work.

remove the stop block and cut out the waste on both top joints.

4. Rotate your miter gauge clockwise, setting it to a heavy 57 degrees. Set a stop block on the miter gauge, and cut the shoulder of the lap joint for the bottom joint. Repeat for the second harp leg, then remove the stop block and cut out the waste on both joints.

5. Glue the two harp legs together while they're still square.

6. Now that the bottom joint is finished, mark out and cut the harp shape. Enlarge the illustration on p. 63 to full size or make your own design and trace it onto the workpiece. Cut out the design using a bandsaw or coping saw.

7. Make sure the shoulders of the two top laps are perpendicular. Set the fence on your table saw so you just slightly trim the front shoulder, then flip the harp and trim the other leg (see **photo F**).

8. Measure across the top of the legs of the harp and cut the cross bar to final length.

9. The measurement for the two laps on the cross bar probably won't be identical, since bandsawing out the harp is not an accurate method of making symmetrical parts, so take a measurement for one of the shoulders from one leg of the harp using a combination

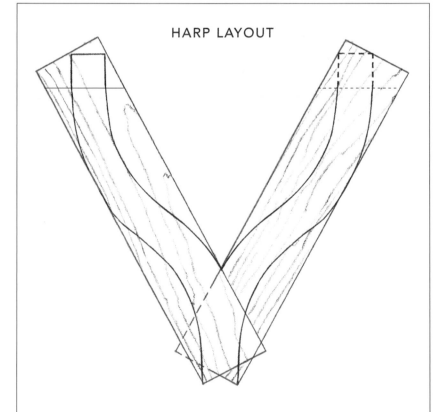

HARP LAYOUT

Glue up the workpieces while they're still square. That way you can glue up across the joint, using the nibs to hold the clamps. The lines of the harp are purely decorative, so don't worry about making them exact. Your only concern is to fit the top bar accurately between the legs. Do this by trial.

square. Transfer it to one end of the cross bar, then repeat the procedure and transfer the measurement to the other end of the cross bar.

10. Set a stop on your miter gauge so that one shoulder on the cross bar is correctly positioned. Cut the shoulder using the dado set (see **photo G**). Reset the stop for the second shoulder, then turn the workpiece around and upside down so that the cut you just made faces up, and cut the second shoulder. Remove the stop and cut out the waste on the two joints.

11. Mark the center of the bottom edge of the cross bar and drill a ½-in. hole there. Fit that hole with a 3-in. by ½-in. hardwood dowel and glue it in place. Fit the cross bar to the harp leg assembly with the dowel facing down and glue and clamp it.

12. When the glue is dry, cut off the two top nibs using a handsaw. Sand the top flush with an 80-grit sanding block.

Photo F: Run the harp against the fence and cut the top shoulders square.

Photo G: Fitting the bar into the opening between the legs is tricky. It's easiest to cut both shoulders until the bar just fits. Use paper shims to microadjust the stop.

Photo H: After you've glued the cross bar to the harp and cut off the nibs, run the cross bar against the fence to cut the harp bottom. This ensures that the bottom is parallel to the cross bar.

Tip: Make sure the pivot holes on the stretchers are facing up.

13. To cut the bottom of the harp, run the top rail of the harp against the table-saw fence, cutting off the bottom. This ensures that the bottom is parallel with the top (see **photo H**).
14. Turn the harp upside down and find the center of the harp bottom. Drill a ½-in. hole into the bottom and fit that hole with another 3-in. by ½-in. hardwood dowel. Glue the dowel into place.

ASSEMBLING AND FINISHING UP

Sanding

Sand the legs, feet, stretchers, cleats, tabletop, and harp to 220 grit, using a random-orbit sander on the flat surfaces and sanding blocks on the curves. Start with a belt sander on the tabletop, using a 150-grit belt, then finish up with the random-orbit sander. Break all of the edges using a sanding block so the edges are comfortable to touch.

Assembling the trestle

The top stretcher must be inserted through the harp before the trestle assembly is glued up. If you forget, you won't be able to get the harp on. As usual, doing a dry glue-up will prevent problems from arising when you're gluing for real.

1. Assemble both leg structures dry to make sure everything fits together properly. Use waxed paper between the leg and glue blocks so the blocks don't stick to the leg, and dry-clamp the assembly to make sure you have everything in order.
2. Spread PVA glue into the foot mortises on one leg structure and then onto the tenons on the leg. Insert the tenons, then clamp the structure, making sure all the joints are tight. Repeat for the other leg structure.
3. Measure for square across the diagonals and correct any deviation.
4. Spread glue into the four leg mortises and onto the stretcher tenons. Insert the stretcher

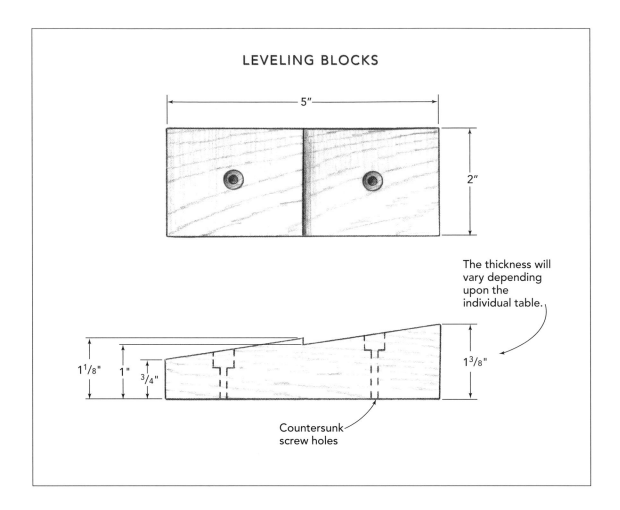

LEVELING BLOCKS

5"

2"

The thickness will vary depending upon the individual table.

$1^{1}/_{8}$" 1" $^{3}/_{4}$"

$1^{3}/_{8}$"

Countersunk screw holes

tenons into one of the leg structures and hammer them home using a dead-blow hammer.

5. Place the harp, which is already assembled, through the top stretcher.

6. Insert the tenons into the second leg and clamp the structure, using clamp blocks on both sides of the exposed mortise to get good clamp pressure. Make sure the trestle sits square on a flat surface. If it doesn't, adjust the clamp pressure.

7. Remove excess glue and allow the glue to cure overnight.

8. Remove the clamps and, using a sharp chisel, chamfer the edges of the exposed tenons, which should show about ¼ in. on each side of the legs.

Attaching the cleats to the tabletop

With the trestle complete, you can fit the cleats to the underside of the tabletop. It is easier and faster to do this dynamically than to try to measure them.

1. Set the trestle on the floor, and insert a 3-in. by ¾-in. hardwood dowel through the hole in one of the cleats and into one of the legs. The dowel should stand slightly proud of the surfaces. Cut it to correct length using a handsaw, and chamfer the edges of the dowels slightly using sandpaper or a chisel to make them easy to insert. The dowels should be sized to go in and out of the holes with finger pressure. Sand them to size if needed.

2. Attach the other cleat to the other leg.

3. Turn the tabletop upside down onto your workbench, then put the trestle, with cleats attached, upside down on the overturned tabletop. Prop up the trestle so it doesn't fall over. Center the trestle on the top.

4. Predrill for screws and screw the cleats into the top, using 1½-in. by #10 steel wood screws.

5. Pull out the pivot dowels and remove the trestle. Glue ⅜-in. wooden plugs into the screw holes. When the glue is dry, cut off the plugs, then level using a sharp chisel followed by sanding.

Adjusting the harp

The harp should pivot on the dowels in their holes, rather than resting on the stretchers. You can accomplish this by adjusting the length of the dowels so that when they are seated in their holes they raise the harp slightly above the stretchers.

1. Mount the harp into the holes in the stretchers.

2. Measure the distance between the harp and the stretchers and subtract ⅛ in. The correct dowel length between harp and stretchers is ⅛ in., so you're cutting off the extra dowel length, leaving only the ⅛ in.

3. After taking the harp out of the holes, cut off the amount you calculated from both dowels.

4. Remount the harp. The harp should now be riding ⅛ in. above the stretchers.

5. If the harp doesn't swing freely, sand the dowels with 80-grit sandpaper on a sanding block until it does.

Leveling the table

The final step is to install the leveling blocks and level the tabletop in relation to the trestle. Rough dimensions for the leveling blocks are given in the illustration on the facing page, but the final dimensions should be calculated dynamically from the finished table.

1. Remount the trestle on the tabletop, which should still be upside down.

2. Pivot the harp so it is perpendicular to the legs, and use shims to level the trestle until the two legs of the harp are equidistant from the bottom of the table. Measure that "leveling distance," which corresponds to the 1-in. measurement shown in the illustration on the facing page. If your measured leveling distance is greater than 1 in., add the difference to the thickness of the leveling block. If it is less than 1 in., subtract that difference.

3. Make two leveling blocks at the calculated thickness. Bandsaw out the slopes and sand them smooth with 80-grit paper and a sanding block.

4. To test the fit, flip the tabletop level, pivot the harp open, and put the blocks into place. The blocks will be held in place for the moment by the pressure between the tabletop and harp. If the block is too thin, add a piece of veneer or cardboard between it and the table; if it's too thick, plane off the bottom.

5. Position the blocks and predrill for the two screws, making sure to countersink the heads. Then glue and screw the blocks to the bottom of the table with 1½-in. by #10 steel wood screws.

Finishing

Traditionally, vineyard tables were often unfinished, though some had oilcloth covers held on with a strip of wood tacked to the edge. (If you see nail holes around the edge of an antique vineyard table, you'll know what they were for.) A tung oil finish gives this table a natural look while still protecting it from the elements. If you've made the table from scrap or multiple species of wood, you might want to paint it. Milk paint (see Sources of Supply on p. 183) followed by oil will create a period look. See appendix 1 on pp. 178–179 for details.

EXPANDING RECTANGULAR TABLE

This project introduces the expanding table—a better solution than a knockdown table for occasions when you have more guests than usual or want to serve dinner more formally.

Stephen Brandt of New Cumberland, Pennsylvania, built this table for a client who had already ordered a set of Windsor chairs. The Queen Anne style of the table suits the chairs, and Stephen designed an elegant mechanism to expand the table to its full size. Unlike most expansion tables, this one doesn't have broken aprons. Instead, the tabletop splits and slides along the apron to accommodate leaves.

More precisely, slides attached to the tabletop sections ride in grooves cut into the apron. The leaves expand the table by a total of 24 in. Closed, it seats six informally; with leaves, it seats eight.

The table's turned cabriole legs give it its 18th-century flavor. You wouldn't think this kind of leg could be turned on a lathe, but the techniques of off-center turning allow you to turn these and many other unlikely looking pieces. Woodworkers without lathes can substitute the traditional carved cabriole leg shown on p. 122.

Expanding Rectangular Table

THE RECTANGULAR EXPANDING TABLE opens in the center to accommodate leaves totaling 24 in. The aprons remain intact while L-shaped slides attached to the tabletop ride along grooves cut into them. The end aprons are notched to accommodate the extension supports, which have knobs on the end for easy operation. Queen Anne–style legs are made by off-center turning on a lathe.

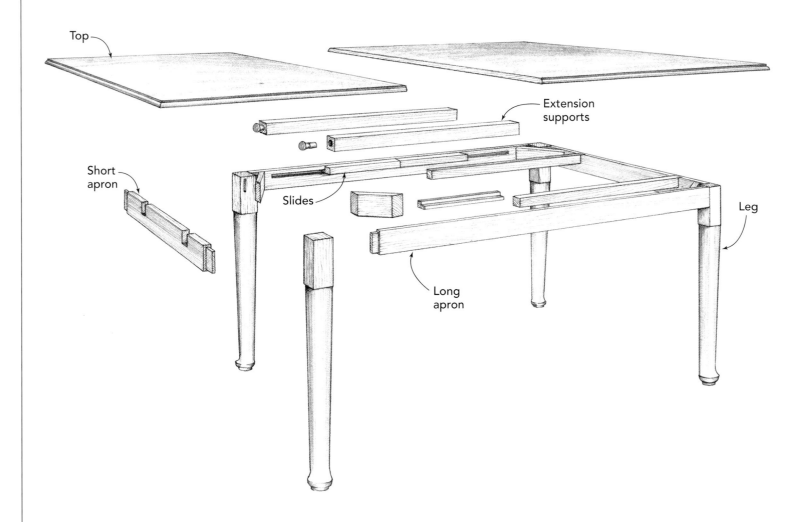

Top

Extension supports

Short apron

Slides

Leg

Long apron

TOP VIEW

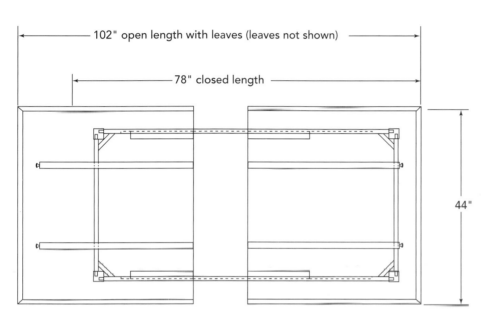

102" open length with leaves (leaves not shown)

78" closed length

44"

CORNER DIMENSION DETAIL

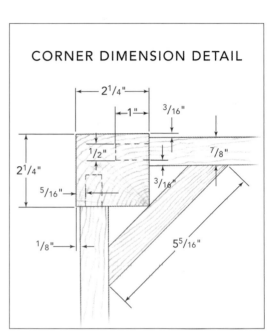

$2^1/4$"

1"

$3/16$"

$7/8$"

$1/2$"

$2^1/4$"

$5/16$"

$3/16$"

$1/8$"

$5^5/16$"

SIDE VIEW

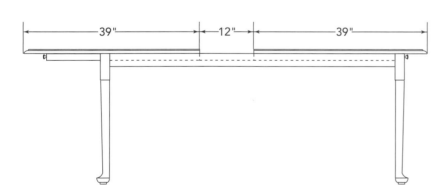

39"

12"

39"

END VIEW

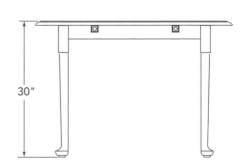

30"

BUILDING THE TABLE STEP-BY-STEP

CUT LIST FOR EXPANDING RECTANGULAR TABLE

Tabletop and Leg Assembly

2	Tabletops	44 in. x 39 in. x ⅞ in.
2	Leaves	44 in. x 12 in. x ⅞ in.
2	Short aprons	31½ in. x 3 in. x ⅞ in.
2	Long aprons	65½ in. x 3 in. x ⅞ in.
4	Corner blocks	5⁵⁄₁₆ in. x 3 in. x ⅞ in.
4	Legs	29⅛ in. x 2¼ in. x 2¼ in.

Expansion Mechanism

4	Extension supports	34⅛ in. x 1½ in. x 1½ in.
4	Extension support knobs	1⅜ in. x ¾ in. x ¾ in.
4	Slides	14 in. x 1½ in. x 1¹¹⁄₁₆ in.

Hardware

44	Wood screws	2 in. x #10
8	Wooden alignment pins	1 in. x ⅜ in. diameter (4 pins per leaf)

This table presents several challenges. The leaves must be integrated into the tabletop so it looks and feels like a single piece. There should be no breaks in the grain pattern, the table edge, or the surface of the tabletop. The expansion mechanism must also be carefully constructed and fitted so the table will open easily without racking or binding. Finally, the cabriole legs require careful attention.

PREPARING THE STOCK

Milling the lumber

1. Decide how you will mill the boards for the leaves based on your jointing capacity. The total width of the leaves is 24 in. If you have a 12-in. jointer, make two leaves. If you have less than a 12-in. jointing capacity, either make three smaller leaves or make two 12-in. leaves by ripping wide boards in half, jointing and planing each half separately, and gluing the halves together again.

To achieve a consistent thickness, plane the boards for tabletops and leaves at the same time, using the same planer settings. In a table with leaves, the thickness of the tabletop is a critical dimension. Even a slight mismatch between level of the tabletop and leaf can cause a wineglass to tip over when it hits the lip.

2. Using scrap wood for the extension support knobs, rip the scrap to 4/4 square and 8 in. long on a bandsaw. Don't bother jointing or planing the piece.

3. If you are making the carved legs, use 16/4 stock or glue up your blanks from the same board to get a good color match. Joint only the two edges that become the back of the leg. Plane the blank minimally, keeping as much wood as possible for the knee. The blank must sit square so you can cut the mortises.

Gluing up

Integrating the leaves into the tabletop is a challenge. Ideally, the tabletop should be well matched both open and closed. If you have to compromise, choose the best match for the closed position (you'll probably use the leaves on formal occasions when you can cover any mismatch with a tablecloth). But try to get the best match you can for both configurations.

1. Once you have chosen the boards for the tabletop and expansion leaves, lay them out and arrange them in the order you want for the top (see "Matching Lumber" on pp. 19–21).

2. Glue up the two tabletop sections, and glue the leaves back together if you've split them. Don't skimp on clamps; if you don't have enough, glue up one section of the tabletop at a time. Allow the glue to dry overnight.

Cutting to dimension

1. Rip both tabletop sections to width, then crosscut them to length. Keep in mind that the grain goes across the table, not lengthwise. Make sure the two halves are exactly the same length so they will meet up properly when pushed together. Measure each section for square across the diagonals.

2. Cut the leaves to length, making sure they are exactly the same length as the tabletop sections.

Preliminary sanding

Plane, scrape, and sand the top to flat only up to about 150 grit. Avoid sanding the edges too much—you need to keep the edge thickness uniform for the edge treatment. Sand the bottom of the tabletop only enough to get out the mill and construction marks (100 grit), except for a few inches around the edges, which should be sanded to 220 so anyone reaching under the table will feel a finished surface.

MAKING LEGS

Cutting and mortising

1. Square one end of each leg, then set a stop on the table saw and cut all of the legs to the same finished length.

2. Lay out and cut the mortises, using a mortising machine or router setup.

Turning the legs

Historically, cabriole legs were hand-carved, with a knee extending from the table and a foot underneath. Producing them was slow and required a competent journeyman. Turned cabriole legs, which are unique to Queen Anne-style work, were used only for the rear legs of cabinets. Since the turned legs had no knee, the cabinets could be pushed flush against the wall. These legs could be produced quickly, and the cabinetmaker saved the expensive work for the public side of the cabinet.

Today, fancy turning is its own reward. If you can turn standard single-axis spindles competently, off-center or multi-axis turning is

a good place to begin expanding your turning vocabulary. The sidebar on p. 78 explains the theory behind the technique.

Practice on a piece of scrap before cutting into your "money wood." (If you prefer not to turn the legs, you can make carved cabriole legs using the patterns shown in the illustration above. Instructions are given on pp. 127–129.)

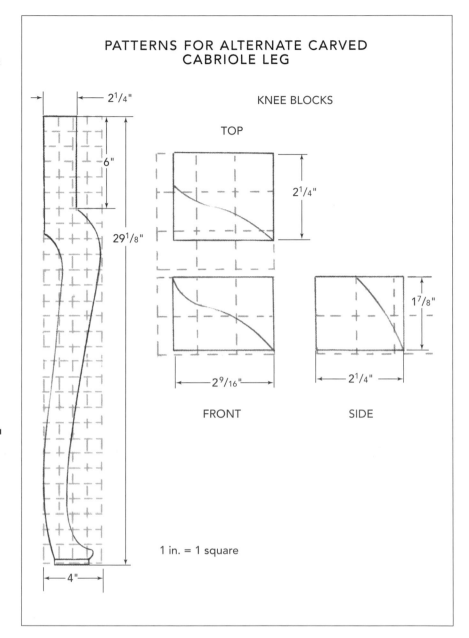

PATTERNS FOR ALTERNATE CARVED CABRIOLE LEG

KNEE BLOCKS

TOP

FRONT   SIDE

1 in. = 1 square

OFF-CENTER TURNING

Tip: In theory, you should move the pommel end of the blank in the opposite direction from the foot so that the original and new axes of rotation cross at the shoulder. In practice, this isn't necessary. Fudge the line around the pommel and no one will notice.

Off-center turning is a lot of fun and surprisingly easy. It works because turning is symmetrical around the axis of rotation. Always start by turning the piece on center. Illustration "A" shows the result, with the leg turned to round and the foot defined. Then move the tailstock slightly off the original axis, as shown in "B," and remove the waste, as shown in "C."

How far you move the axis is up to you—the farther you move it, the thinner the leg will be at the bottom. Moving the headstock in the same or opposite direction shifts the placement of the leg in relation to the pommel and expands the range of possible shapes.

Remember that during half of each revolution there is no material under the tool and all you will see is a ghost (shown in "D"). You can't "rub the bevel" to make this cut. To quote the great turner Richard Raffan, "Imagine your line and go for it." Don't push; let the wood come around to the tool edge.

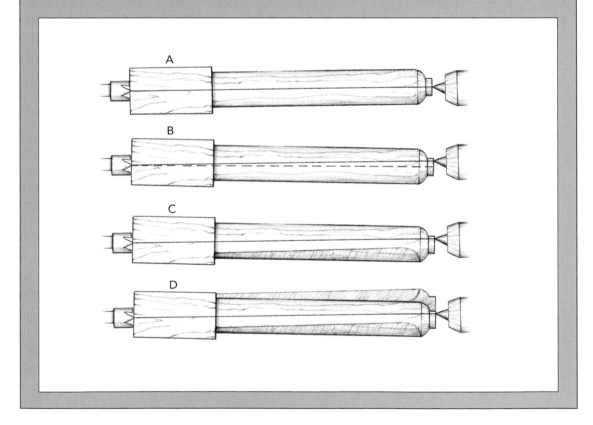

Photo A: Use calipers and a parting tool to size the diameter of the foot, then turn it with a gouge.

1. Mark the position of the shoulder and mount the blank with the pommel (the mortised end) toward the headstock.

2. Using a pair of calipers and a diamond-shaped parting tool, determine the major diameter next to the shoulder.

3. Cut the shoulder and turn the blank to round down to the major diameter.

4. Mark the position of the foot, then use calipers and a parting tool to size it. Turn the foot and sand it to 220 grit (see **photo A**).

5. Move the foot end of the blank ⅞ in. toward the inside edge of the leg so that the foot splays outward at a 45-degree angle to the table. If there isn't enough wood to seat the center ⅞ in. off the original centerline, screw a piece of scrap plywood to the bottom of the leg before repositioning the blank.

6. Finish turning the foot and then turn the rest of the blank. When the ghost disappears, the blank is round and you can stop turning.

TURNED LEG DETAIL

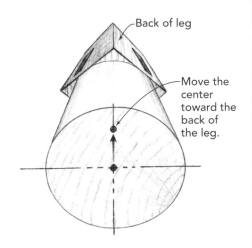

Back of leg

Move the center toward the back of the leg.

This figure, shown without the foot cuts, shows how to move the center so the foot points into the room. If you moved the center in the opposite direction, the foot would turn inward; if you moved it to the side, the foot would be backward or pigeon-toed.

Tip: Be sure to wear eye protection while you're turning. I prefer a full-face mask.

Photo B: Power-sanding long curves is very fast and gives clean results.

7. Sand the leg on the lathe using a power-sanding disk to 220 grit (see **photo B**).
8. If necessary, clean up the foot with a rasp before turning the lathe back on and hand-sanding the top of the foot.
9. Repeat for the other three legs.

JOINERY OPERATIONS

Cutting the grooves

After cutting the aprons to length, use a router bit and router table to cut the grooves in the long aprons. (If you don't have a router table, use a fence on a hand-held router.)

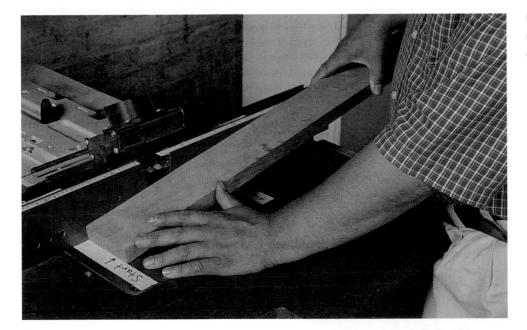

Photo C: Aligning the pencil marks shows you when to start and stop the cut.

1. Tighten a ¾-in. straight bit into the collet of the router, and mount the router. If it has adjustable speeds, set the speed to medium.
2. Adjust the router table fence so its inside edge is ¾ in. from the bit.
3. Mark "start" and "stop" points for cutting the grooves. The grooves should be exactly opposite each other so the tops won't rack when you open them. If you have a long enough fence, simply set a stop on it. If not, position the first apron so its end is 4¾ in. ahead of the front of the bit. Tape the board to the fence, draw a pencil line across the tape, and cut it using a mat knife. Label the tape on the fence "start." Now position the apron so its end is 4¾ in. behind the back of the bit. Repeat the tape-marking procedure, labeling the second piece of tape "stop." Mark the second apron similarly (see **photo C**).
4. Align the pencil mark on the first apron with the "start" line.
5. Holding the board tight against the fence, plunge the board down onto the tabletop and the spinning bit. Using push sticks or fingerboards to hold it in position, push it through the bit, stopping when the "stop" mark is aligned with the mark on the apron.
6. Repeat for the second long apron.
7. Raise the router bit to ¹¹⁄₁₆ in. and repeat the cut for both aprons.

Photo D: Squaring the ends of the grooves makes a positive stop for the slides when the table is closed.

8. Using a combination square set to 4¾ in. and a marking knife, mark both ends of the groove. Position a ¾-in. mortising chisel on the knife mark, and whack the chisel hard with a mallet to square the ends of the grooves (see **photo D**).

Photo E: Notice that
the half-fence stops
before the blade
begins. It's an easily
adjustable stop for
repetitive cuts.

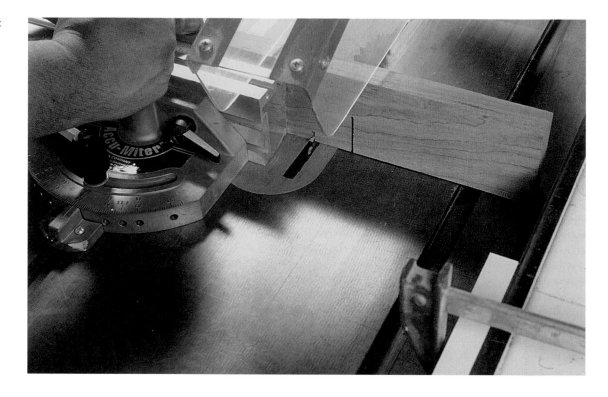

Cutting openings for extension supports

The slides are operated by pulling on extension supports that run under each section of
the tabletop and through the short aprons.
The openings in the aprons should be slightly
larger (a heavy $\frac{1}{32}$ in. wider and higher) than
the cross section of the extension supports
so that seasonal wood movement doesn't
bind them.

1. Lay out one opening using a combination
square and marking knife. The opening should
be slightly larger than $1\frac{1}{2}$ in. wide by $1\frac{1}{2}$ in.
deep and should start 6 in. from the end of
the apron.

2. Put a dado set onto the table saw. Normally
the widest dado you can set up for is $\frac{3}{4}$ in., so
it will take two cuts to make each opening.

3. Position the apron so the dado set cuts the
knife line (the resulting slot should be slightly
oversized), and set a stop on your miter gauge.
Clamp a half-fence made from scrap onto your

table-saw fence to act as a position finder. The
half-fence should end just before the dado
blade begins. Position the apron, then move
the half-fence and fence to it. Lock the fence.
You can position subsequent cuts by abutting
the apron against the half-fence (see **photo E**).

4. Raise the dado set so it is below the final
level. If you have a basket guard, remove it for
this operation.

5. Position the apron and make the first cut.
Raise the dado set until you just cut through
the depth line.

6. Next, flip the apron around and make the
first cut in the opposite slot.

7. Make the cuts on the other short apron.

8. Reposition the fence and half-fence so that
the inside mark will be cut away, and repeat
the steps to cut the second half of each slot.
Clean up any waste with a sharp chisel.

Cutting the tenons

Finally, cut the tenons, using a tenon jig as
described on p. 34.

Expansion Mechanism

THE SLIDES THAT RUN in a groove cut into the long apron should be slightly undersized so seasonal wood movement doesn't cause them to bind. Make sure the slides are quartersawn along the horizontal axis and the aprons are also quartersawn, since quartersawn lumber moves less than flatsawn. The slides should be finished to minimize the exchange of moisture and then lubricated with paste wax.

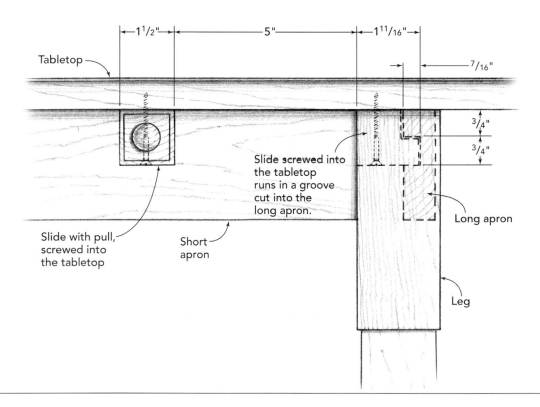

Tabletop

1½" — 5" — 1¹¹/₁₆"

⁷/₁₆"

³/₄"

³/₄"

Slide screwed into
the tabletop
runs in a groove
cut into the
long apron.

Slide with pull,
screwed into
the tabletop

Short
apron

Long apron

Leg

MAKING THE EXPANSION MECHANISM

Making the slides

The slides are sections of hardwood with a rabbet cut in one side to make an L shape. This creates a tongue that slides in the grooves previously cut in the aprons. You'll need a sacrificial fence attached to your rip fence to bury the dado head.

1. Start by marking a line on a piece of scrap ¾ in. from the edge. Clamp the scrap to the fence.

2. After lowering the dado set, position the sacrificial fence over the throat-plate opening. Be careful not to place the actual fence over the opening.

3. Raise the dado until it just cuts the line at ¾ in.

4. Position the fence so that only ⁷/₁₆ in. of the dado is showing. Now you're ready to cut the rabbet in the slides.

5. Use a featherboard to hold the slide blank against the fence and a push stick to push it through the dado set.

6. Drill three screw holes in each slide. Two of the three holes should be oversized and elongated along the length of the slide to accommodate seasonal wood movement, since the slides are screwed to the tabletop cross-grain. Unless you elongate the holes, seasonal wood movement could crack the top.

EXTENSION SUPPORT KNOB

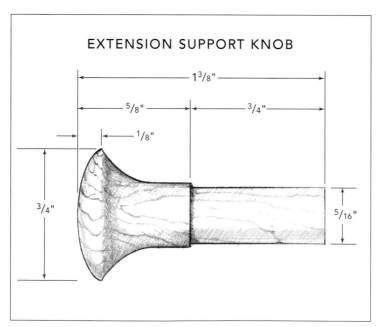

1³/₈"

⁵/₈"

³/₄"

¹/₈"

³/₄"

⁵/₁₆"

Turning the knobs for the slides

The knobs are turned from scrap. Turn one knob after another, parting each one off as you go, then recentering the blank and turning the next one. This requires a blank about 1 in. in diameter and 8 in. long. Or, if you prefer, just cut four 2-in. blanks and turn them separately. You'll need one pair of calipers set to ¾ in., one pair of dividers set to ⅜ in., and a ⁵/₁₆-in. open-end wrench for the tenon.

1. Mount the blank on the lathe with the tenon facing the tailstock and turn it to round.
2. Using the dividers against the spinning work, place the right arm of the dividers at the midpoint of the blank and measure ⅜ in.
3. Using a diamond-shaped parting tool and the open-end wrench, part down to establish the tenon's shoulder. Remove the waste to make the tenon, sizing it with the wrench (see **photo F**).
4. Hold the parting tool to the right of the mark that shows the front of the knob, and part down until the calipers slip over the spinning work. The width of the parting tool establishes the width of the knob's face.

Photo G: Once the knob is free, it stops turning immediately. Cradle it in your hand as you part it off with the skew. If you prefer, leave a ⅟₁₆-in. connection, then stop the lathe and saw off the knob.

5. Turn the back of the knob with a small gouge, leaving enough to establish a shoulder next to the tenon.

6. Use a skew chisel to turn the front of the knob. Just before the knob parts off, sand the spinning work to 220 grit. Part the knob off cleanly with the skew, cradling it in your hand so it doesn't go flying (see **photo G**).

7. Continue until you have four pulls.

Making the extension supports

1. Cut the extension supports to length.

2. Draw diagonals on one end to find the center point, and mark that point with an awl.

3. Clamp the workpiece and mount a ⁵⁄₁₆-in. brad-point bit into your drill. Mark off 1 in. on the bit with masking tape, and drill a hole in one end of each of the four supports, stopping when you reach the masking tape. Drill straight so the knob will sit evenly with the surface of the extension support.

4. For detailing, chamfer the end of the support. Cut the chamfer with a sharp chisel and sand it with a sanding block.

5. Drill four screw holes in each extension support. Three of the four should be elongated, like the holes you drilled in the slides, to accommodate the seasonal wood movement of the top.

ASSEMBLY AND FINISHING UP

Sanding

Sand all of the remaining parts except the tabletop to 220 grit. With a sanding block and 220-grit paper, break all the edges.

Leg assembly

1. Glue the short aprons to the legs, checking for square across the diagonals. Leave the assemblies in clamps for a few hours.

2. Glue the long aprons to the leg assemblies and check for square across the diagonals. If the apron assembly is not square, the expansion mechanism will bind.

3. When the glue is dry, attach the corner blocks, following the method shown on p. 39.

Tip: When you are parting off, do not wear rings or long sleeves that could catch the workpiece.

Slides

The slides attach the tabletop to the leg assembly, in addition to serving as the expansion mechanism.

1. Start by placing a protective blanket on your bench or other flat surface.
2. Turn the two tabletop halves upside down. Clamp the halves together from below, using clamp blocks so as not to mar the edges.
3. Place the leg assembly upside down on the top and center it, then clamp it into position so it can't move in relation to the top.
4. Insert the slides into the grooves in the aprons, and align them with the joint between the two halves. Use a dime on either end of the slide between it and the apron to position the slide relative to the apron. Mark for the screws using an awl. Remove the slides and, using a ⁵⁄₆₄-in. drill bit, drill the tabletop for the screws. Finally, replace the slides and screw them to the tabletop.

Extension supports

The extension supports must be screwed to the tabletop parallel to the aprons and slides or they will bind when the table is expanded.

Photo H: This commercially available doweling jig centers itself onto the edge of the board and accepts different size drill bits. Align the mark on the board with the mark on the jig.

1. Glue the pulls into the extension supports, cleaning up the excess glue with hot water and a rag.
2. Insert the extension supports into their holes, aligning the chamfers with the outsides of the apron openings.
3. Next, put one screw in each support at the end closest to the apron, predrilling for the screw.
4. Expand the tabletop on the bench. Since one end of each extension support is screwed down, the hole in the apron will now align with the other end. Drill for and insert the remaining screws.
5. Place the table right side up on the floor.

Table alignment pins

This table uses wooden alignment pins to align the parts of the tabletop (see Sources of Supply on p. 183 for where to find alignment pins).

1. Clamp the tabletop and leaves together on a flat surface, using two bar clamps at least 9 ft. long. (You can buy extensions for standard bar clamps or longer lengths of pipe if you're using pipe clamps.) Make sure the top surface is level and the ends meet, and use clamp blocks on the ends so as not to mar the edges. With the tabletop clamped, you can measure for the table pins and their holes quickly and accurately.
2. Using a pencil and a combination square set at 4 in., mark across the joints where the top meets the leaves and the leaves meet each other. If you have two leaves, you should have six marks; with three leaves, eight marks.
3. Clamp a block at the 22-in. mark of a yardstick. Use the block as a stop, measuring 22 in. into the middle of the table. Running a pencil across the end of the ruler, make a mark across the three leaf joints. Stay on the same side of the table so the leaves will be interchangeable.
4. On the left side of every joint, mark an X. On the right side, mark an O. The pins will be on the X sides and the holes for the pins on the O sides.

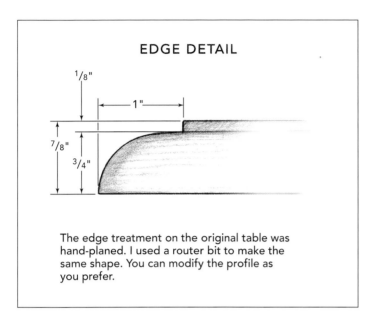

EDGE DETAIL

1/8"

1"

7/8"

3/4"

The edge treatment on the original table was hand-planed. I used a router bit to make the same shape. You can modify the profile as you prefer.

5. Unclamp the table and separate all of the leaves.

6. Mount a drill bit with the same diameter as the pin's tenon.

7. Aligning a self-centering doweling jig over one of the X marks, drill the hole. Repeat for the rest of the X marks (see **photo H**).

8. Change the drill bits to one that is the same diameter as the head of the pin, and drill the O holes using the doweling jig.

9. Glue the pins into the X holes and clean up excess glue with hot water and a rag.

Edge treatment

1. Reassemble the table, inserting the table pins into the pinholes, then reclamp the table-top across its length. The clamps will keep the edges from tearing out when you cut across the joints.

2. Mount the router bit for your edge treatment in your router. If you're using a plunge router, adjust the depth and set the stop.

3. Clamp a long straightedge just far enough from the edge that the router base will run against it, jigging the cut. Rout the end grain (long side) first so any tearout at the ends will be removed when you rout the ends of the table. Take care not to let the guide bow in the middle when you apply pressure. Routing end grain is tough; take shallow passes, lowering the bit each time. Run the router left to right.

4. Once you're satisfied with the edge, move the straightedge to the other side of the table and repeat the process.

5. Move the straightedge and cut the edge treatments on both ends.

6. Sand the edge treatment to 150 grit. If you sand with the clamps on, you won't round over the edges. When you're finished sanding, remove the clamps.

Final sanding and finishing

1. With the leaves in the table, finish sanding the tabletop and edge detail to 220 grit using a random-orbit sander.

2. With a 220-grit sanding block in one hand, go over every inch of the table, looking for blemishes and dings you may have missed.

3. Finish the table. The original table was finished with wiping varnish. See appendix 1 on pp. 178–179 for finishing instructions.

Expanding Racetrack Oval Table

This beautiful racetrack oval table designed by John Lomas, the owner of Cotswold Furniture Makers in Whiting, Vermont, uses a more traditional expansion mechanism than the rectangular table on p. 72. In this table, as in most expanding tables, both the top and the aprons break apart to create an opening for leaves. When closed, the table is round and seats four. With all three leaves in, it seats eight comfortably. Lomas makes this table in cherry and offers optional edge and apron treatments. For an even more formal piece, mahogany or walnut would be good choices.

Several new techniques are introduced in this project. The two half-round aprons are built using a bent-lamination process. Bent lamination can be done in several ways, but the method I show here uses clamps and a caul over a form. The legs and apron are joined with a half-bridle joint, a strong way to attach legs to a continuous apron. Finally, the front profile of the legs is belt-sanded; Lomas' shop, like most professional woodworking shops, uses a belt sander to shape curves whose dimensions are noncritical.

The biggest challenge in this table is making the leaves interchangeable. If you follow the steps in the sequence shown, you'll produce three identical leaves and won't have to remember which leaf goes where every time you put them in.

Expanding Racetrack Oval Table

THE EXPANDING RACETRACK OVAL TABLE seats four when it is closed and eight when all three leaves are inserted. The two halves of the tabletop slide apart with their aprons to make room for the three leaves and their aprons. Four legs are joined to the round apron by half-bridle joints, and a removable fifth leg in the center provides stability when the table is opened.

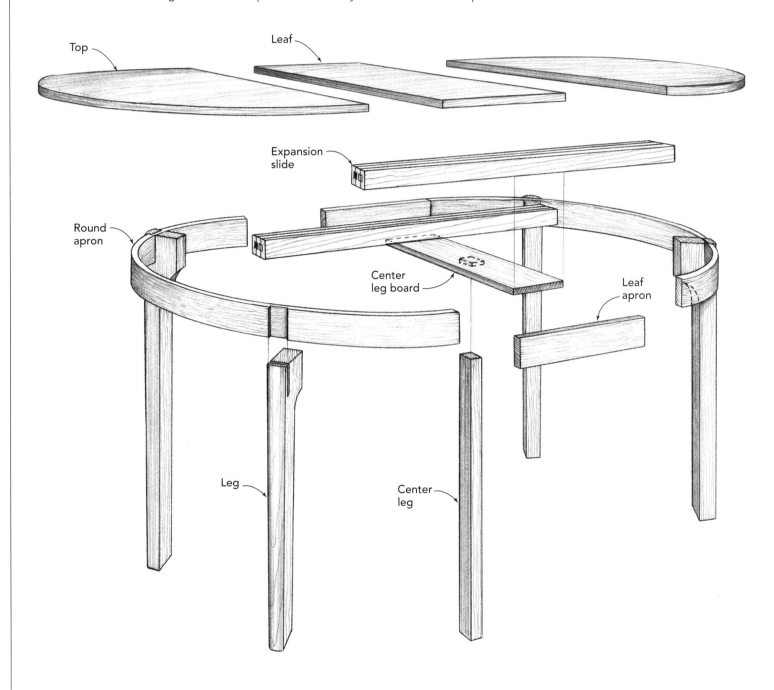

Top

Leaf

Expansion slide

Round apron

Center leg board

Leaf apron

Leg

Center leg

TOP VIEW

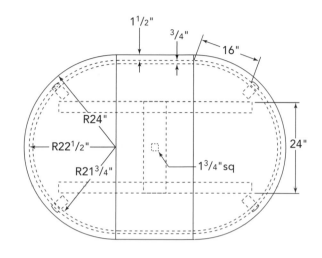

$1\frac{1}{2}$"
$\frac{3}{4}$"
16"
24"
R24"
R22$\frac{1}{2}$"
R21$\frac{3}{4}$"
$1\frac{3}{4}$"sq

SIDE VIEW

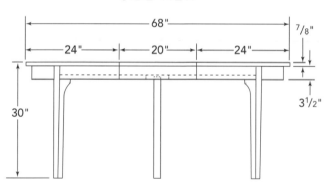

68"
24"   20"   24"
$\frac{7}{8}$"
30"
$3\frac{1}{2}$"

END VIEW

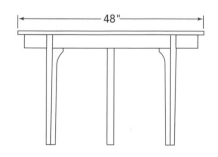

48"

LEG DETAIL

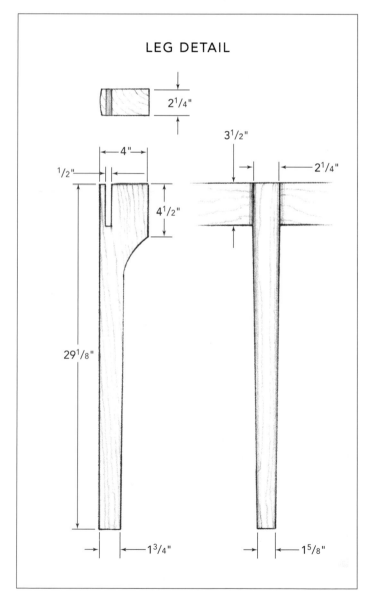

$2\frac{1}{4}$"
$3\frac{1}{2}$"
4"
$2\frac{1}{4}$"
$\frac{1}{2}$"
$4\frac{1}{2}$"
$29\frac{1}{8}$"
$1\frac{3}{4}$"
$1\frac{5}{8}$"

BUILDING THE TABLE STEP-BY-STEP

CUT LIST FOR EXPANDING RACETRACK OVAL TABLE

Tabletop and Leg Assembly

2	Tabletops	48 in. x 24 in. x 1 in.
2	Round aprons	2 sheets ⅛-in. bending ply, to wrap around a 4-ft. cylinder 7-ft. x 4-in. cherry laminations (2 per apron)
3	Leaves	48 in. x 20 in. x 1 in.
6	Leaf aprons	1 sheet ¾-in. birch ply 21-in. x 4-in. cherry laminations (2 per apron)
4	Legs	29⅛ in. x 4 in. x 2¼ in.
1	Center leg	Approx. 28 in. x 1¾ in. x 1¾ in.
1	Center leg board	24 in. x 10 in. x 1 in.

Hardware

34	Desktop fasteners	
34	Steel wood screws	1 in. by #8
34	Steel wood screws	½ in. by #8
12	Steel wood screws	Size depends on thickness of expansion slides
2	Expansion slides	60 in.
12	Alignment pins and sleeves	
8	Table locks	
1	Tee nut and leveler	

Shop Materials for Bent-Lamination Process

1	Sheet of tempered Masonite for cauls
1	Sheet of 1-in. shop birch for bending form

After gluing up the tabletop, the first step in building this table is to make the round aprons using a bent-lamination process. Bent lamination isn't difficult, but it is time-consuming; if you don't want to spend the time, you could use commercially available precut aprons. Only after the aprons are finished and their mortises cut can you make the legs, attach the expansion hardware, cut the tabletop to round, and cut the leaves to length. Finally, the hardware is added to the leaves so that they can be fitted and locked into the table.

MAKING THE PARTS

Preparing the stock

1. Select boards for the tabletop and leaves that will match well.

2. Mill the outside legs ⅛ in. wider than their final width. You will adjust the width after cutting the apron mortises.

3. Use the ⅛-in. bending plywood for the interior and the ⅛-in. cherry laminating veneer for both faces of the apron (see Sources of Supply on p. 183). Milled veneers save work and expense and are available in sequential leaves that match in color and grain (see **photo A**).

You should cut the bending plywood and the veneer at least ¼ in. oversize—you'll cut the apron to final width after it's glued together (see **photo B**). Joint one edge of the veneer before ripping it to width. Although this veneer is thick enough to cut with a table saw, you'll need to back it up to make it easier and safer to control. You can use scrap or, in this case, the tempered Masonite you use for cauls. With the fence still set, rip the bending plywood to get 14 strips.

4. For the plywood leaf aprons, cut the cherry laminate surface layers ½ in. oversize.

Photo A: To size the veneer to length, first score it with a mat knife, then snap it off.

5. To cut the plywood for the leaf aprons, crosscut the plywood sheet into six strips each 5 in. wide, then rip a 22-in. piece from each. This may seem like a waste of plywood, but it results in pieces with the grain running in the short direction. See "Balanced Panel Construction" on p. 99 for an explanation of why you should do this.

Building the tabletop

Glue up the tabletop's two halves and three leaves as you did for the expanding rectangular table on p. 76. Remember that on tables with expansion leaves the grain runs across the table—that is, parallel to the straight edges. Try for a good grain match across the entire surface, whether the leaves are in or out. If you have to compromise, choose the best match for the configuration that will be used most. Sand to 150 grit, but don't cut the top to round yet.

Photo B: Rip the veneer slightly oversize using a plywood backing board. First, tape the veneer to a piece of scrap, then joint one edge. Set your fence to at least ¼ in. over the width, reverse the board so that the jointed edge runs along the fence, and rip the veneer.

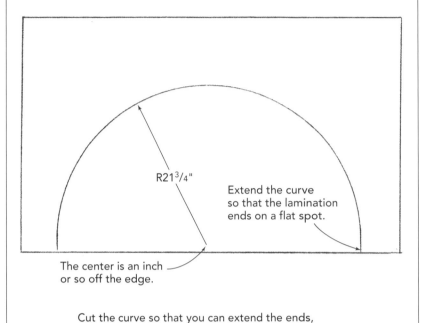

CUTTING THE APRON BENDING FORM

R21¾"

Extend the curve so that the lamination ends on a flat spot.

The center is an inch or so off the edge.

Cut the curve so that you can extend the ends, creating flat spots where the lamination can end.

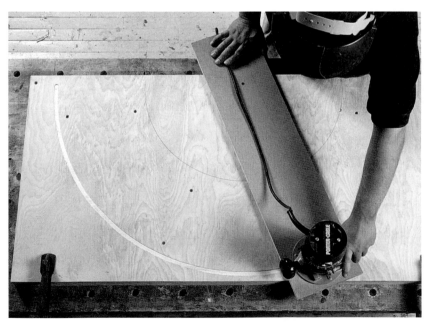

Photo C: Using the trammel as a jig, rout out the circle in several passes so as not to overtax the bit.

Building the apron-bending form

The form used to make this apron is semicircular and 4 in. thick and is built up by gluing four 1-in. birch plywood half-circles together. You will use a plunge router attached to a pivot as a trammel to cut the half-circle shape. The pivot is a piece of scrap 3 ft. by 8 in.

1. Mount a ½-in. bit in your router, then remove the baseplate and screw the router to one end of the pivot. Clamp the pivot with the router hanging off of the side of the bench so you don't cut into the bench, and plunge the bit through the scrap.

2. Screw the pivot to the plywood at its other end. To mark the point of attachment, unplug the router, measure 21¾ in. from the inside edge of the bit, and mark the point with an awl. Drill through this point with a small-diameter drill bit.

3. Crosscut the plywood into four equal pieces, each 48 in. long and 23⅞ in. wide (the saw kerf removes ⅛ in.). Put two of the pieces on the bench and clamp them where the pivot won't hit them, then screw the two pieces together with a drywall screw at each corner.

4. Screw the pivot to the plywood so the diameter of the half-circle will run about 1 in. from the edge of the plywood, as shown in the illustration at left above. Using several passes, rout through the first layer and slightly into the second (see **photo C**).

5. With a large compass, trace another half-circle with the same center and a 13¾-in. radius. Later you will cut out this half-circle so the inner edge of the form can serve as a clamp surface.

6. Next, remove the clamps and screws. Cut off the rectangular area below the half-circle with a table saw or handsaw. Using the completed first layer as a pattern, trace the pattern onto the remaining layers and bandsaw out the waste. On each layer, use a large compass or a pencil, string, and nail to lay out the 13¾-in. half-circle as well.

7. Glue and screw the pattern layer to one of the other layers, placing the screws away from the inner half-circle line. You will need glue to resist the pressure exerted by the clamps used for the bent lamination. The screws simply act as temporary clamps until the glue cures.

8. Mount a flush trim bit into your router and trim the second layer to the first. Glue and screw the third layer to the first two and rout it flush. Continue the process with the fourth layer.

9. Bandsaw out the inside circle, but be careful—the form is heavy. A second set of hands is helpful.

10. Screw scrap to the bottom, making sure there is no overhang onto the form. These feet allow you to clamp the form securely so it won't topple when loaded.

11. Run your hand over the form to feel for any highs or lows, then fair the form using a random-orbit sander and 80-grit paper. Fill any dip with automotive body filler and sand the curve to fair it. Finally, cover the outside of the form with plastic packing tape or waxed paper and spray adhesive so the lamination won't stick to it. Let the form stand overnight so the glue can cure fully before you use it (see **photo D**).

Making the round aprons

The round apron is built using the bending form as a foundation for the bending plywood and the cherry laminate. In effect, you're making plywood, except that it's curved rather than flat (see "Balanced Panel Construction" on p. 99). If you're proficient with a vacuum bag, you can use that in place of clamps.

Since this is a complicated glue-up requiring many clamps, you should do a dry glue-up first.

Photo E: Urea resin cures by a chemical reaction. If you wrap the excess glue in a bag, you'll know it's time to remove the clamps when the glue in the bag is hard enough to crack.

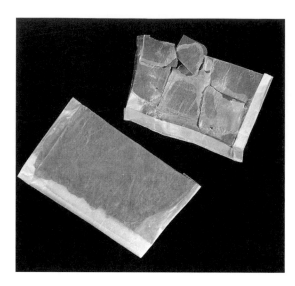

1. Wearing your protective gear, mix the urea resin glue.

2. Build up the apron using one strip of cherry, seven strips of bending ply, and then one last strip of cherry. Spread glue on top of each layer (except the final one) as you put it down, and tape the lamination lightly with masking tape to keep the layers together.

3. After spreading a piece of waxed paper over the lamination, place the tempered Masonite strips on top to be used as cauls. Use pieces of scrap on top of the cauls to distribute clamp pressure across the width of the lamination. You need even pressure all over the lamination to make the curve fair, without dips and bows.

Photo F: This lamination required more than 40 clamps. Any clamps will do—use bar clamps if you need to—as long as you use enough to apply even pressure to the lamination. The cauls distribute the clamp pressure evenly.

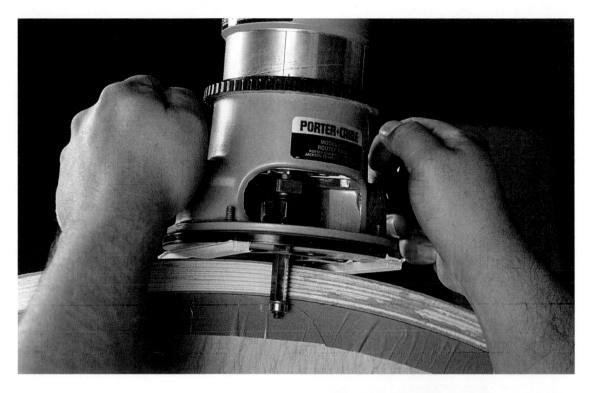

Photo G: Two runners attached to the router base with double-faced tape provide a solid footing and prevent the router from rocking during the cut.

4. Tape the assembly together with masking tape and transfer it to the form. Clamp the midpoint, then work your way out toward the ends. Since the inside radius of the aprons is shorter than the outside radius, the ends of the plies won't match.

5. Spread a little leftover glue on waxed paper, fold the paper over, and seal it. Unlike PVA, which cures by evaporation, urea resin cures by chemical reaction. Since that reaction is heat sensitive, its timing varies with shop temperature. When the glue in the paper is brittle, release the clamps and glue up the second half (see **photos** E and F).

6. To trim the apron to size, first joint one edge. Since the edge of the form is perpendicular to its curved side, you can use the form itself as a pattern. Make sure the form is clean, and scrape off any dried glue. Position and clamp the apron so it hangs just off the side of the form. Make sure it's square to the form, then joint with a router and flush trim bit (see **photo G**).

7. Although cutting the apron to width is awkward, you can use a table saw with a good plywood blade (see **photo H**). A safer but

Photo H: Use a high-end veneer plywood blade (high-angle alternate top-bevel/ 80+ tooth) and zero-clearance throat plate to rip the lamination to final width. Otherwise you'll get tearout on the bottom or public edge. Use the blade guard.

Photo I: A small planer does a good job on bent laminations, but take shallow passes through the planer and support the work along its length.

slower method is to put the apron through the planer (see **photo I**).

8. Trim the apron to length, then put the apron back on the form and mark both ends. Use a chopsaw to trim the ends to length while supporting the assembly with a triangular shim to get a square cut (see **photo J**).

9. Sand, if necessary. If the clamp pressure was not exactly even, the apron curve may not be fair. Since the veneer is so thick, you can usu-

ally sand your way out of trouble using a random-orbit sander and 80-grit paper.

10. Repeat these steps for the second round apron.

Making aprons for the leaves

1. To build up the apron, use one strip of cherry, one strip of finish plywood, and then one or more strips of cherry. Spread glue on the plywood, put the veneer on top, then turn

Photo J: Trimming the ends takes careful preparation. Use a shim to square and support the end of the apron to the chopsaw blade.

BALANCED PANEL CONSTRUCTION

A lamination consists of a central panel, or core, with an equal number of veneers or plies on either side of it. To achieve balanced construction, place the outer layers in pairs of equal thickness and of the same species. Most furniture-grade plywood has a poplar core with veneer on the outside faces. If you add another layer of veneer to one side, add a second layer to the opposite side to maintain balanced construction. This is true even if you veneer over MDF or particleboard.

The rule is: "What goes on one side must go on the other."

Even though veneer is very thin, it's still wood. Like solid wood, it expands and contracts across the grain when the humidity in the air changes. Crossbanding—placing each layer with the grain at 90 degrees to the grain in the previous layer—stabilizes a straight laminated panel. (This is why the plywood strips for the leaf aprons are crosscut.)

Photo K: Use large cauls and enough clamps to distribute the clamp pressure evenly across the surface of the workpiece. Otherwise you'll get bubbles where the veneer isn't attached.

the workpiece over. Again spread glue on the plywood, and place the veneer on top.

2. Put a piece of scrap sheet goods down on your bench, and cover with a piece of waxed paper. Place the workpiece on top, then cover it with another layer of waxed paper, another piece of plywood, and a thick piece of scrap over everything to act as a final caul. Clamp the assembly (use plenty of clamps) and let the glue cure. When the glue is dry, joint one edge and rip to final width (see **photo K**).

Cutting the open mortises

1. Measure a 16-in. chord from one end of one of the aprons, as shown in the top view illustration on p. 91 to determine the placement of the near side of the leg, and clamp the jig as shown in the illustration on p. 102 to the apron. Using a ½-in. downward spiral bit and corresponding guide bushing, rout out the

GLUE FOR LAMINATIONS

While PVA has been adequate for all of the solid-wood work we've done so far, the glue of choice for lamination and veneering is a two-part urea resin such as Unibond 800 (see Sources of Supply on p. 183).

PVA is inadequate for bent lamination because it cures to a semirigid state. This is fine for joinery, where you want a little "give" to accommodate seasonal wood movement. But bent laminations have a natural tendency to straighten themselves out, and rigid glue is needed to counteract that "springback" tendency. In addition, urea resin has an open time of up to an hour, an advantage in complicated glue-ups.

The glue comes in two parts, a liquid resin and a powdered hardener, with directions for mixing. I usually need to mix one and a half times the recommended amount. The glue should be the consistency of thick cream—a cookbook would say it "coats the back of a spoon." Spread it evenly until running your finger across the glue makes a nice line. I use an old credit card, followed by a paint roller with a short nap. You can buy rollers especially for glue.

Since urea resin is poisonous, always use rubber gloves, a respirator, and eye protection when mixing and using it. Clean up with cold water. Since urea resin cures with heat, hot water will harden it immediately and you won't be able to get it off.

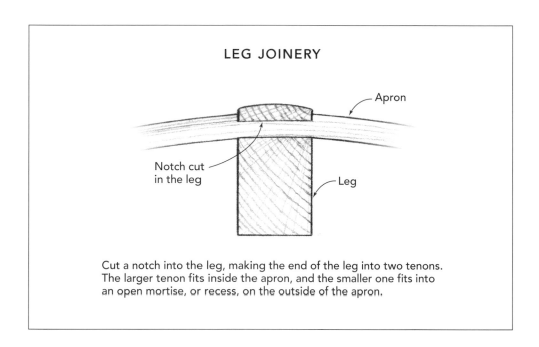

LEG JOINERY

Apron

Notch cut
in the leg

Leg

Cut a notch into the leg, making the end of the leg into two tenons.
The larger tenon fits inside the apron, and the smaller one fits into
an open mortise, or recess, on the outside of the apron.

waste down to 1 in. from the top of the jig
(see **photo L**).

2. Cut the other three open mortises in the
same way.

MAKING THE LEGS

Making the center
leg joinery

1. To calculate the thickness of the center leg
board, subtract the thickness of the expansion
slides from 3½ in. The center leg board should
be as thick as possible (accommodating as
long a tenon as possible and therefore making
the center leg as stable as possible) without
showing below the apron. Don't make the
board thinner than ¾ in.

2. Mill the center leg board to its calculated
thickness.

3. Mark the midpoint of the board, then lay
out and cut a 1¾-in.-square mortise using a
router. The mortise shouldn't go through the
board, only about ½ in. into it. Square up the
mortise using a chisel.

4. Calculate the length of the center leg as follows: 30 in. minus the thickness of the tabletop, minus the thickness of the expansion
slides, minus the thickness of the center
board, minus the thickness of the leveler,

**Photo L: Guide bushings come in many sizes. They take the place of
a bearing on the router bit, allowing any bit to be used for pattern
routing.**

A Mortising Jig for the Apron

This mortising jig provides a stable platform and a pattern to run a router with a guide bushing. It has a fence to reference the apron and has angled supports that rest against the curved apron surface and provide a convenient place for clamps. It works by providing a router-guide window that's the size of the mortise plus the offset for the guide bushing.

1. To make the outer pieces, rip a 4-in.-wide strip of ¾-in. MDF and cut two 10-in. pieces from the strip.

2. For the crosspieces, first calculate the width of the mortise opening, then rip a strip of MDF to that width and cut the two 2½-in. crosspieces off the strip. The width of the mortise opening equals the width of the finished leg—2¼ in.—plus the width of the guide bushing, minus the width of the router bit. With a ½-in. router bit and a ⅝-in.-wide bushing, the opening would be 2¼ in. plus ⅝ in. minus

½ in., or 2⅜ in. Since the width of guide bushing varies, measure your bushing and do your own calculation.

3. Biscuit-join these pieces together on a flat surface.

4. Make the fence and biscuit-join it to the jig, perpendicular to the opening in the jig and aligned with the edge of the crosspiece.

5. Cut a 1⅝-in. strip for the legs of the jig. (In theory the legs have to be only 1½ in. long in order for the jig to sit on the apron on three points, but in practice that's tricky to accomplish. It's better to make the legs a little long so the jig doesn't rock, and shorten them later.) Cut the legs and biscuit-join them to the edges of the jig. Miter the top of the leg with your table saw at a 14-degree angle. If your blade tilts to the right, attach a temporary fence to your table-saw fence with double-faced tape so the blade won't hit your fence.

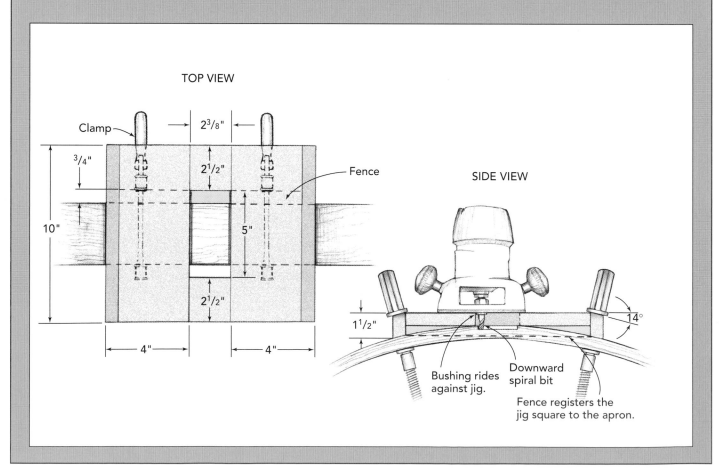

TOP VIEW

Clamp

2³/₈"

3/4"

2¹/₂"

Fence

SIDE VIEW

10"

5"

2¹/₂"

4"

4"

1¹/₂"

14°

Bushing rides against jig.

Downward spiral bit

Fence registers the jig square to the apron.

minus ⅛ in., plus the depth of the mortise cut into the center board.

5. Cut the center leg to ¹⁄₃₂ in. over final width and thickness, then sand or scrape it to fit into the mortise you've cut in the center leg board.

6. Finally, cut the center leg to length. Predrill for the tee nut, then drive the tee nut into the bottom of the leg. Screw the leveler to the tee nut. The foot can be adjusted to make the center leg the same length as the others if the floor is uneven.

Making the outside leg joinery

First, you'll cut the notch into the top of the leg to match the apron mortise, then you'll plane the leg to finished width for a tight fit.

1. Cut the four outside legs to length.

2. Using a tenon jig, first cut the outer edges of the notch on all four legs, then readjust the jig and cut the inner edges so the joints are a little tight. Cut out the waste in multiple passes.

3. Readjust the tenon jig, sneaking up on the exact width, to cut the notches to width.

4. Pass the legs through the planer, testing the fit until the outer leg tenon is about ¹⁄₃₂ in. too wide for the open mortise in the apron, then sand the parts until you get a good fit. Try this on a piece of scrap first.

Shaping the legs

1. To cut the side tapers, use the taper jig described on p. 32. Since these legs, unlike the legs on the kitchen table on p. 22, have opposing sides tapered, you will need two jigs. For the center leg, which has all four sides tapered, cut two adjacent sides with one jig, then the other two with the second jig.

2. To make a pattern for the back curve on the outside legs, enlarge the illustration for the leg detail shown on p. 91 to full size and paste the drawing to a piece of scrap. Cut out the curve and fair it with a file and sandpaper.

3. Lay out the curve on the rear of the legs using the pattern. Use one of the cutoffs from the tapers to level the leg when you cut out the curve with a bandsaw or coping saw. This will make the curve square in relation to the rectangle the legs were cut from.

4. Clamp the legs to the table and sand out the curve using a belt sander.

5. Using a table saw, cut a ⅛-in. chamfer from the two front edges. Repeat for the other legs. On the center leg, chamfer all four sides.

6. Clamp the legs to your bench and sand both of the tapers. Then flip the legs and use a belt sander to sand delicately over the chamfer so the fronts of the legs are gently rounded. On the center leg, round over all four chamfers.

ASSEMBLING AND FINISHING UP

Assembling the table

When assembling this table, you'll first glue the outside legs to the apron using PVA glue. Clamp both top to bottom and across the joint for a tight fit.

The tabletop is attached to the apron with steel figure-eight-shaped desktop fasteners that permit seasonal wood movement. One fastener loop is screwed down into the apron while the other is screwed upward into the tabletop (see Sources of Supply on p. 183).

1. Adjust a lightweight plunge router to the depth of the fasteners. Mark attachment points and rout out recesses for about eight fasteners on each round apron. Predrill and screw the fasteners to the aprons with 1-in. by #8 wood screws.

2. After placing a blanket on top of your bench, turn one-half of the tabletop upside down. Position the apron on the tabletop, preserving the half-round shape. Using a pair of trammel points, lay out a half-circle on the underside of the table to align the apron.

3. Clamp the apron in place and mark out, predrill, and screw the fasteners to the top with ½-in. by #8 wood screws.

4. Repeat with the second half of the table.

Fitting the tabletop parts

1. Use alignment pins to align the two halves of the table. Since you haven't yet cut the tabletop to shape, use the apron as a reference point for placing the pins. On one half of the tabletop, mark the two points where the apron ends. Now find and mark the midpoint between those two marks, which will be the center of the table. Unscrew and remove the apron.

2. Abut the two tabletop halves and mark the second side from the three marks made in step 1. Using a self-centering doweling jig, drill for and insert the table pins at all six marks (see pp. 86–87 for detailed instructions). Put the pins in one half of the tabletop and the sleeves in the other.

3. To install the locks that hold the structure together, clamp the two halves of the table together and clamp the whole structure to the bench so it lies flat. Mark out, predrill, and install the table locks on the inside of the apron. Once again, measure from a known reference point, such as the mark you made for the pins. Test the locks and leave them locked.

4. Use wooden expansion slides to support the leaves (see Sources of Supply on p. 183). Position the slides on the underside of the table while it's clamped up. The outsides of the slides should be 2 ft. apart and centered on the centerline. The two slides should be parallel to each other and perpendicular to the table's centerline. The slides screw into the table—follow the directions that come with them. Mark with an awl for the screws, then predrill and attach the slides.

5. Position the center leg board on the middle sections of the slides, which hang down below the two outer sections. Since the middle slide

Tip: On a solid-wood tabletop, use the router only to trim off the final ¹⁄₁₆ in. Do not cut out the circle with the router.

sections remain in place when the table opens, the center leg will stay centered. Mark, predrill, and screw three screws into the middle section of each slide.

Cutting the tabletop

Cutting the tabletop to round has been postponed until now so you could match up the halves perfectly. With the pins and locks installed, you can now mark out the circle and cut it.

1. Remove the apron, slides, and center leg and lock the tabletop halves together. Using a set of trammel points with a pencil substituted for one point, mark out a 48-in.-diameter circle on the bottom of the tabletop. Use the center mark you made for the alignment pin as your center for the circle.

2. Unlock the tabletop halves and cut out the circle to within ¹⁄₁₆ in. of the line with a bandsaw, jigsaw, or coping saw.

3. Make a quarter-circle pattern from MDF, position it, and clamp it to the tabletop. Using a flush trimming bit, trim off the final ¹⁄₁₆ in. You'll need to climb cut, or run the router right to left, on half of the circle (see "Climb Cutting" on the facing page), so that the clockwise-spinning bit always moves "downhill" and won't tear out the wood. When you rout across the break, lock the two table halves together so they will support each other and not cause tearout across the break.

Making the leaves

The leaves should be identical so they can be installed in any order. To make them identical, work on one leaf at a time.

1. Reassemble the table and stand it on its legs, then open the table and insert one leaf. Using the pins in the table halves as a guide, mark the positions of the leaf pins, then drill holes and install the pins. Clamp across the table to install locks on the leaf, and lock the leaf in place.

CLIMB CUTTING

Climb cutting, or moving the router bit right to left as you face the work, produces very clean results if done properly. However, because you're moving the router in the same direction the bit is turning, the bit has a tendency to grab the workpiece and pull itself along. This can be dangerous and hard to control. For this reason, climb cutting is used for cleanup purposes only.

Use a sharp bit and climb cut only small amounts of material—no more than 1⁄16 in. Be sure to use only a handheld router, and never, ever climb cut on a router table or shaper without using a power feeder—you can lose your fingers and hands.

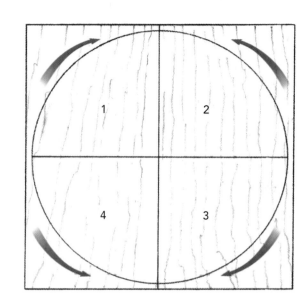

To minimize tearout along the edge, climb cut (run the router from right to left) in quadrants 1 and 3. In quadrants 2 and 4, run the router from left to right. If you're putting an edge treatment on the table, make it in several shallow passes.

2. Measure and cut to length the aprons for the leaf you're working on. The leaf aprons should be 1⁄16 in. narrower than the leaf to allow seasonal wood movement.

3. Make mortises for, predrill, and screw three desktop fasteners into each of the leaf aprons, then replace the leaf in the table and lock it in. Clamp the apron in place, leaving 1⁄32 in. on each end. Take the leaf out of the table and turn it over. Mark for, predrill, and screw the apron up into the leaf.

4. Repeat the steps to install the pins, locks, and aprons for the other two leaves.

5. Install one leaf, then mark out and cut it to length. Make sure the short edges are perpendicular to the long edges, or the leaves won't be interchangeable.

6. Repeat with the other two leaves.

Finishing

Sand all exposed surfaces to 220 grit and finish with tung oil varnish (see appendix 1 on pp. 178–179 for finishing information).

EXPANDING PEDESTAL TABLE

The graceful Morris/Olvis Dining Table® was designed by Ambrose Pollock of Carmel, California, for a client whose house was designed by a student of Frank Lloyd Wright. The tripod design solves one of the biggest problems of expanding pedestal tables, which is that central pedestals may be unattractive when they are broken into two halves. This pedestal works equally well with the table open or closed.

I've chosen this table to demonstrate modern woodworking techniques. Traditional joinery, glues, and materials have their devoted adherents, some of whom disapprove of modern methods. In my experience, however, woodworkers who use modern products and techniques correctly and who understand wood movement can produce results at least as durable as those produced by traditional methods.

In this project, I'll show how to use a biscuit joiner for solid-wood joinery. Although it isn't traditional, biscuit joinery can be very strong. Research has shown that double biscuits, used properly, can be nearly as strong as mortise-and-tenon joints in solid wood. They're certainly strong enough for this application. Biscuit joinery is also very fast and accurate, an advantage not only for production woodworkers but also for the hobbyist with limited time to spend in the shop.

Expanding Pedestal Table

THE EXPANDING PEDESTAL TABLE opens on wooden slides to accommodate three leaves. The pedestal consists of two tripods that fit together when the table is closed. Each tripod is made from three identical sections, two butted together and the third joined at right angles to the other two. Biscuit joinery is used for all of the pedestal joints. The expansion slides fit through notches cut into the pedestal cleats.

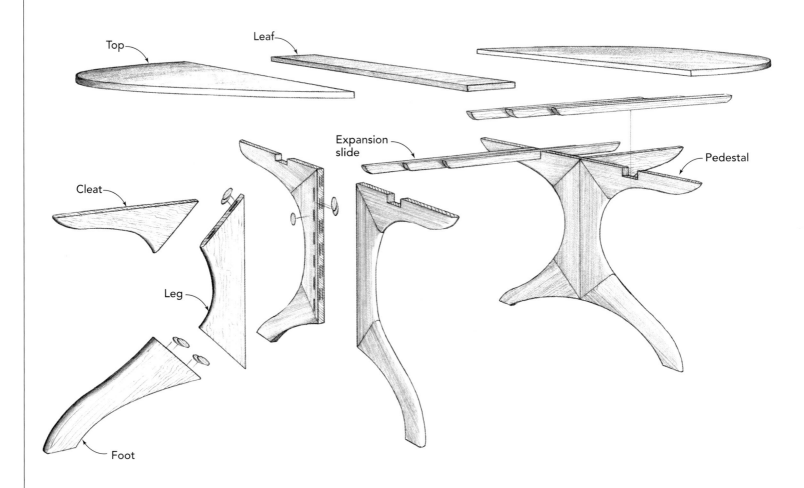

Top

Leaf

Expansion slide

Pedestal

Cleat

Leg

Foot

TOP VIEW

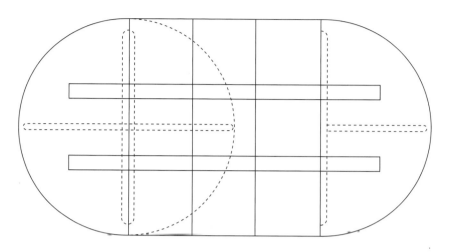

SIDE VIEW

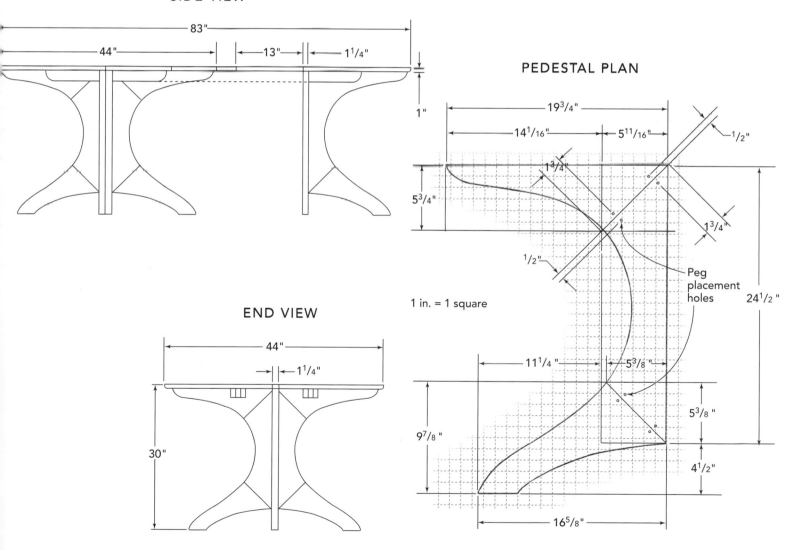

83"

44"

13"

1 1/4"

1"

PEDESTAL PLAN

19 3/4"

14 1/16"

5 11/16"

1/2"

1 3/4"

5 3/4"

1 3/4"

1/2"

Peg
placement
holes

24 1/2"

1 in. = 1 square

END VIEW

44"

1 1/4"

30"

11 1/4"

5 3/8"

5 3/8"

9 7/8"

4 1/2"

16 5/8"

BUILDING THE TABLE STEP-BY-STEP

CUT LIST FOR EXPANDING PEDESTAL TABLE		
Tabletop and Leg Assembly		
2	Tabletops	44 in. x 22 in. x 1 in.
3	Leaves	44 in. x 13 in. x 1 in.
6	Pedestal cleats	19¾ in. x 5¾ in. x 1¼ in.
6	Pedestal legs	24½ in. x 5¹¹⁄₁₆ in. x 1¼ in.
6	Pedestal feet	16⁵⁄₁₆ in. x 9⅞ in. x 1¼ in.
Hardware		
2	Expansion slides	42 in. expanding at least 39 in.
36	Desktop fasteners	
16	Alignment pins and sleeves	
8	Table locks	
100	Biscuits	#20
16	Wood screws	2 in. x #8
36	Wood screws	1 in. x #8
36	Wood screws	½ in. x #8
Decorative Elements		
48	Ebony or cherry pins	2 in. x ¼ in. x ¼ in.

This table is simple to make and, if you use biscuit joinery for the pedestal and follow the sequence of operations given here, you should be able to put it together quickly.

The tabletop is glued up and rough-cut to a rectangular shape, then the pedestal parts are joined and their curves are bandsawed out and sanded using patterns. Installing the expansion hardware, cutting the tabletop to round, cutting the leaves to final length, making the edge treatment, and adding the leaf hardware should be postponed until after the pedestal has been completed and attached to the tabletop.

MAKING THE PARTS

Milling the lumber

The only critical dimension for milling is the thickness of the boards. The pedestal boards must be the same thickness, even if that isn't precisely 1¼ in., and the tabletop boards must also be the same, even if their thickness isn't precisely 1 in.

1. Cut all of the boards to rough length, leaving the top boards about 4 in. long. Also leave the cleats and feet a little long to allow room for error.
2. If you're starting from rough lumber, face-joint one face and edge-joint one edge for each board.
3. To achieve uniform thickness, pass all of the boards through the planer at the first setting, then lower it and pass all of the boards through at the next setting until all boards are 1¼ in. thick. Set aside the pedestal boards and keep planing the tabletop boards until they are 1 in. thick.
4. Rip the boards to width. On the boards you will use for the tabletop, edge-joint the edge coming off the saw.

Making the tabletop

1. Glue up the tabletop's two halves and three leaves with the grain running parallel to their longer sides. Try to match the grain across the entire surface, whether the leaves are in or out. If you have to compromise, choose the best match for the configuration that will be used most often. Let the glue dry overnight.
2. When the glue is dry, rip the two tabletop halves to 1 in. over final width. Joint one edge on each half, then crosscut to length, leaving 2 in. more than the final length.
3. Rip the leaves to final width and crosscut them, again leaving 2 in. more than the final length.

Cutting the mitered edges on the pedestal pieces

The pedestal has six sections, each made of three pieces (cleat, leg, foot) butt-joined together. The sections are joined into two tripods, forming T shapes in plan view. The top of each T is made from two sections butted together. A third section is joined at right angles to the other two.

1. Set your miter gauge to 45 degrees or use a sliding compound miter saw. Set a stop and cut one end of each cleat and each leg to 45 degrees.

2. Holding the triangular cutoff against the stop (see **photo A**), cut the other ends of the legs to 45 degrees.

3. Cut off the corners of the feet to the measurements shown in the Pedestal Plan illustration on p. 109 so that the mitered ends of the feet will match the mitered ends of the legs.

BISCUIT JOINERY

As usual, lay out and cut your joinery before cutting the curves on the pedestal parts. After you lay out the slots, set the biscuit joiner and cut the slots in the ends of all of the pieces and the backs of the legs. Then reset the joiner and cut the slots in the sides of the legs.

Marking the biscuit slots on the mitered edges

1. Stack all of the pedestal legs one on top of the other and stack the cleats on top of them, with all of the miter points aligned. Clamp the pile onto your bench.

2. Using a combination square set to 2½ in., run a pencil along the top of the square while it rides down the miter points. This marks all 12 boards with a line 2½ in. from the miter points (see **photo B**).

Photo A: Using the cutoff against the stop ensures that you'll get a consistent length.

Photo B: Using the corners of the workpieces as your reference edge, run your pencil against the combination square as it slides down the stack.

*Tip: Once you've
marked the biscuit
slots, the legs are no
longer symmetrical.
Be sure to mark the
tops and bottoms of
the legs so you don't
get confused.*

3. Reset the combination square to 6 in., and
mark a second line down the boards.
4. Repeat the process using the feet and the
other ends of the legs, marking lines at 2¼ in.
and 5½ in. from the miter points on the legs.
This is trickier, since the foot's mitered edge
doesn't end in a point. Mark the top board,
then turn the combination square 90 degrees
and use it as a straightedge, referencing off
the top to mark the remaining boards (see
photo C).

Marking the biscuit slots along the backs of the legs

1. Stack the legs with their tops oriented in
the same direction and clamp them to the
bench. Number them as shown in the illustration below and, using a combination square,
mark lines on the long edges at 2¼ in., 5⅛ in.,
8 in., and 10⅞ in. from both miter points.
2. Put an X through every other mark on
legs 1 and 2. On legs 3, 4, 5, and 6, X out the
marks that were not X-ed out on legs 1 and 2.
The X's mark where you *won't* cut slots on the
backs of the legs. Interleaving the biscuit slots
leaves enough material for a sound connection
when you make the right-angle joint.
3. Unclamp and separate the legs and, using a
combination square, extend the marks without
X's onto both faces for about 1 in.

Cutting biscuit slots on the mitered edges and the backs of the legs

1. With the biscuit joiner set to size 20, lower
the fence to 90 degrees and position it so the
center of the slot is ⅜ in. below the fence.
2. Clamp two boards at right angles to your
bench to act as stops for the workpiece (see
photo D).
3. Place the workpiece against the stops.
Holding the fence against the face of the workpiece and aligning the cut mark with the reference mark on the joiner, cut the slot.

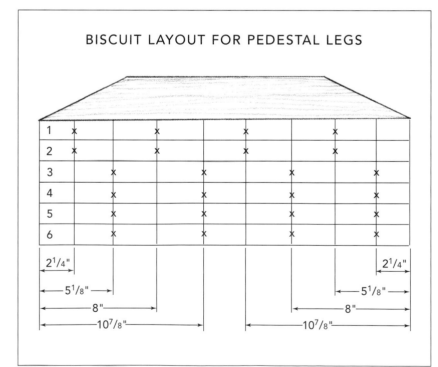

BISCUIT LAYOUT FOR PEDESTAL LEGS

Tip: *Don't try to reference off the bottom of the joiner—the fence is much more accurate.*

Tip: *Never hold the workpiece to the joiner with your hand. Clamp the workpiece or use stops on the bench if you need help keeping it steady.*

Photo D: It's faster to clamp two boards as stops than to clamp each workpiece to the bench individually.

4. Repeat for the remaining slots, then turn the workpiece over and cut the second row, using the opposite face as your reference edge. Don't cut slots where you've marked an X.
5. Repeat for the remaining workpieces, reclamping your stops if necessary. At the end of this process, you will have four biscuit slots on each of 24 mitered surfaces and eight on the back of each leg, for a total of 144 slots.

Cutting biscuit slots on the sides of the legs

For the right-angle joint, you'll cut one row of slots along the sides of legs 3, 4, 5, and 6, using the X'ed-out marks you have so carefully laid out and been equally careful not to use. Be especially careful in this step—if you make a mistake here, you'll need to remake the part.

POSITIONING BISCUITS

$3/8$"

$1^{1}/4$"

$3/8$"

A biscuit slot is about $5/32$ in. wide, so a $1^{1}/4$-in. board has plenty of room for a double row of biscuits with enough wood between and around them to make a strong joint.

BISCUIT JOINTS

A biscuit joint is equivalent to a floating tenon joint. Biscuits can be used wherever a floating tenon or spline joint would be used. However, standard gluing rules still apply. Glue joints are strong only where long grain meets long grain. (This includes the 45-degree cuts in the pedestal parts, which have enough long grain to make a strong glue joint.) End-grain-to-end-grain and end-grain-to-long-grain glue joints should be avoided. Biscuits always work well with sheet goods, which have enough long grain to be glued together in any configuration. With solid wood, you must keep in mind the limitations of biscuits just as you would the limitations of other joints.

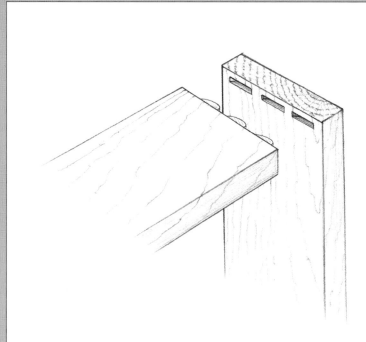

This solid-wood configuration is unsound for biscuit joinery, since all of the glue surfaces in the slots of the vertical board are end grain, and glue does not work well with end-grain joinery. The other three possible ways to orient the boards will work fine.

1. For these slots, use the back edge of the leg as your reference edge (see **photo E**). Reset your fence to ³⁄₁₆ in. (half what it was in the previous setup) and make test cuts in two pieces of scrap. If the joint is not correct, make microadjustments by putting a piece of paper, folded if necessary, between the work-piece and the fence.

2. When your test cuts are accurate, cut the slots in the sides of legs 3, 4, 5, and 6, aligning the X'ed-out lines with the reference mark on the joiner so the slots will match up with the slots on the backs of legs 1 and 2. Remember that the legs are not symmetrical, so you need to cut the slots for legs 3 and 4 on the opposite surfaces from the slots for legs 5 and 6 so they will end up adjacent to each other when leg 3 is butt-joined to leg 5 and leg 4 to leg 6 (see **photo F**).

Cutting holes for the pegs

The joints in the pedestal are highlighted by decorative square pegs. It's a good idea to cut the holes for these pegs before gluing up the pedestal sections so you can use the drill press. The pegs don't go all the way through the leg. Since the legs are asymmetrical, be careful where you mark for holes. The pegs on legs 3, 4, 5, and 6 should be on the same sides where you've just cut biscuit slots, so they will be visible when the table is closed. The pegs on legs 1 and 2 should be on opposite sides from each other, so they will both be visible from the same end of the table.

1. To mark the peg placements, measure in 1¾ in. from the edge of the joint and ½ in. from the joint itself (see the Pedestal Plan illustration on p. 109). Use an awl to mark the points.

2. Mount a ¼-in. brad-point drill in the drill-press chuck, and position the brad point over the awl mark. Clamp a fence with a stop to your drill-press table and drill all of the holes for that setting, changing your stop as needed. It doesn't matter how deep you drill as long as you don't go through the leg.

Photo E: I constantly find new applications for Mark Duginske's trick of using paper shims to microadjust tooling. Here I use it to adjust the position of the biscuit slot.

GLUING UP PEDESTAL SECTIONS

Gluing miter joints is a challenge because it's hard to get good clamp pressure perpendicular to the joint. I've found one solution that always works: L-shaped cauls that fit over the edge of the workpiece with "teeth" parallel to the joint line. The cauls are easy to make on a table saw or bandsaw. They are clamped to the workpieces, and clamps are then stretched across the joints.

1. Using solid-wood scrap, cut out the two cauls for each joint. On the second cut, leave a sliver attached so the cutoff doesn't kick back. Break off the sliver and clean up with a

Photo F: Before you cut any slots, line up the pieces as they will fit together and mark the surfaces with a witness mark.

Tip: Biscuits are made of compressed birch and expand when exposed to water, making a strong joint. Be sure to use water-based glue for these joints, or the biscuits won't expand properly.

Photo G: This L-shaped caul works to clamp miter joints when all other methods fail.

Tip: Because clamping and unclamping the caul is time-consuming, glue one joint at a time, applying the glue after the caul is in place.

Photo H: The cauls allow clamp pressure to be applied directly across the joint, ensuring a tight fit.

chisel. Cut notches into one leg of the caul at 45 degrees from the edge (see **photo G**).

2. Clamp the cauls to the workpieces for one joint.

3. Using water-based glue (PVA is best) in a glue bottle with a biscuit head, put glue into the slots on both halves of the joint. Place biscuits into one-half of the joint.

4. Put the joint together and clamp across it, applying pressure across the center of the panel so the joint won't rack (see **photo H**). Make sure the peg holes on both pieces are on the same side.

5. Wait for the glue to grab—30 to 40 minutes, depending on the temperature—before taking the clamps off. To save time, make enough cauls so you can continue working as

Photo I: Clamp over and under the assembly to get even pressure across the joint.

you wait for earlier joints to set up. Glue the rest of the miter joints until you have six complete pedestal sections.

Gluing pedestal sections back-to-back

1. Match up pedestal sections 3 and 5 and sections 4 and 6. Each pair should have a double row of biscuit slots along one side.
2. Glue the slots on the backs of these legs, and insert biscuits into half of each joint.
3. Clamp across the joints, as shown in photo I.

FINISHING THE PEDESTAL

Cutting the slots for the expansion slides

1. Measure the width and thickness of the table slides, then transfer those measurements to the four pedestal cleats in the joined sections.

2. Set the height of the table-saw blade to match the depth of the slides.
3. Stand one of the pedestal assemblies vertically, with the cleats down, against the fence of the miter gauge. After positioning it, set a stop, then clamp it to the fence and make the cut. Reverse it and reclamp to make the mirrored cut on the joined pedestal section (see **photo J**).
4. On the second pedestal assembly, make the same two cuts using the same setup.
5. Reset the stop to make the second cut, and use that setting to make all four remaining cuts.
6. Bandsaw out the waste from the four slots and level them using a sharp chisel.

Shaping the parts

1. To make patterns for the pedestal parts, enlarge the Pedestal Plan illustration on p. 109 to full size. Using sprayed contact cement, glue the drawing to a piece of ¾-in. MDF.
2. Bandsaw out the waste for the patterns, leaving just a little over the lines of the draw-

Photo J: Set a stop on the miter gauge and clamp the pedestal assembly to the fence—this is more stable than it looks.

PEDESTAL EDGE TREATMENTS

R^1/$_2$"

R^3/$_4$"

The ^{1}/$_2$-in. roundover on legs 1 and 2 is cut on both sides, while the ^{3}/$_4$-in. roundover on legs 3, 4, 5, and 6 is cut on only one side.

ings, then file, rasp, and sand until you have fair curves. It's worth taking the time to get the curves right.

3. Attach the completed patterns to the first pedestal section with double-faced tape.

4. Using a bandsaw with a pattern-following guide, rough out the first pedestal section. Without removing the patterns, mount a drum sander with a bearing onto the drill press. If the bearing is on bottom, you may need a secondary table on top of the drill-press table for the drum to fit into. Using a coarse-grit drum, sand the pieces flush with the pattern.

5. Repeat for the remaining five pedestal sections.

Cutting the pedestal edge treatment

The edge treatment for the pedestals is a simple roundover. Use a handheld router so you can climb cut sections where the edges

would otherwise blow out (see "Climb Cutting" on p. 105).

Making and installing the decorative pegs

Ambrose Pollock used ebony pegs for this table, but if you don't have access to ebony, any contrasting wood will lend a decorative touch. Even scrap cherry gives a nice contrast because the pegs show end grain.

1. Mill your scrap square, then set your table-saw fence a heavy ¼ in. from the blade. Lower the blade so it is slightly less than ¼ in. above the table.

2. Run the scrap over the blade on all four sides, making eight cuts. Be sure to leave a little sliver of material so the cutoff doesn't kick back (see **photo K**).

3. Break off the workpiece and clean it up with a sharp chisel. Whittle the end of the peg so it fits into the round hole.

Photo K: If you cut off these small pieces, they would be trapped between the blade and fence and kick back. Leaving them slightly attached is much safer.

Photo L: Hammering a square peg into a round hole spreads the fibers of the hole.

4. Put a little glue into the hole, then tap the square peg into the round hole with a hammer until the hole expands to accept the peg (see **photo L**). After the glue dries, cut the peg off just above the surface and sand it smooth with an 80-grit sanding block.

5. Sand all the pedestal sections with a random-orbit sander to 180 grit.

Assembling the tripods

The backs of legs 1 and 2 will be joined to the sides of legs 3, 4, 5, and 6 to form the tripods. Since there aren't any good clamping surfaces, you'll use screws as clamps.

1. Dry-fit one pedestal tripod, using biscuits without glue. Let's assume you are joining leg 1 to legs 3 and 5, which have already been butt-joined.

2. Predrill four 2-in. by #8 screw holes through the side of legs 3 and 5 and into the back of leg 1. Make sure the screw heads will be at least ¼ in. below the surface.

3. Apply glue to the biscuit slots on the back of leg 1, to the entire surface of the back, and to the biscuit slots on the sides of legs 3 and 5.

Insert the biscuits and screw the tripod together.

4. Repeat the process for legs 2, 4, and 6.

5. When the glue is dry, make plugs using your plug cutter and fill the screw holes. Cut the plugs off just above the surface and sand them flush with an 80-grit sanding block.

FINISHING UP

Installing table locks

The table locks need to fit into the 2¼-in. space between the table edge and the pedestal leg. Where you position them depends on their size. Since there is no apron to hide the locks, buy the smallest and lowest-profile locks you can find.

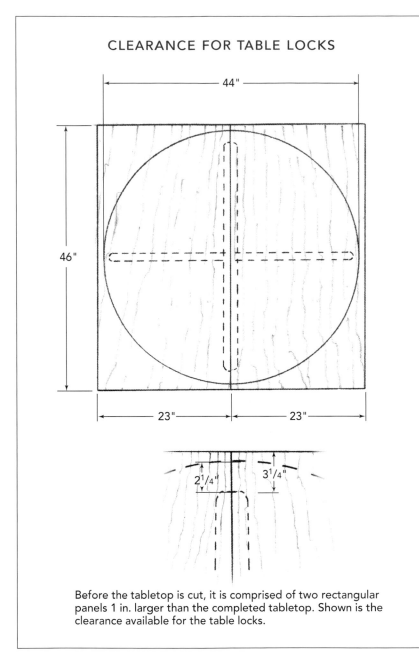

CLEARANCE FOR TABLE LOCKS

44"

46"

23" 23"

2¼" 3¼"

Before the tabletop is cut, it is comprised of two rectangular panels 1 in. larger than the completed tabletop. Shown is the clearance available for the table locks.

1. Place the two tabletop halves upside down on your bench and butt them together.
2. Measure for and install the tabletop locks, paying attention to the clearances.

Attaching the pedestals to the table

The tabletop is attached to the pedestals with steel figure-eight-shaped desktop fasteners that permit seasonal wood movement. One fastener loop is screwed down into the pedestal cleat, while the other is screwed upward into the tabletop (see Sources of Supply on p. 183).

1. Adjust a lightweight plunge router to the depth of the fasteners, then mark attachment points and rout out recesses for six fasteners on each pedestal cleat. Predrill and screw the fasteners to the cleats with 1-in. by #8 wood screws.
2. Turn the pedestal tripods upside down onto the tabletop, equidistant between the table locks.
3. Clamp the pedestals in place with the long sides parallel to the joint between tabletop halves, and mark out, predrill, and screw the fasteners to the top with ½-in. by #8 wood screws.

Attaching expansion slides

1. To support the leaves, use wooden expansion slides (see Sources of Supply on p. 183). Since there is no apron to hide them, round the ends by first bandsawing out a quarter-round on each end, then sanding the ends smooth with a belt sander. Sand the slides and stain them with a couple of coats of cherry stain to hide the color difference. (The slides on Ambrose Pollock's original table are veneered with cherry.) Sand lightly with 320 grit beween coats.
2. Put the slides through the notches in the pedestal cleats.
3. Clamp the slides in place and screw them in.

Installing the remaining hardware

1. With the tabletop and pedestal right side up on the floor, mark for four table pins spaced equally along the edge of the table.
2. Separate the table halves and insert the first leaf, then close the table again and mark the leaf for pins. Repeat for the second and third leaves.
3. Using a doweling jig, drill for and insert the table pins in the tabletop halves and leaves. Make sure you will have alternating rows of pins and sleeves.

4. Turn the tabletop upside down onto your bench, then insert one of the leaves. Clamp the assembly together.

5. Measure for and install the locks on the first leaf, then remove the leaf and repeat for the second and third leaves.

Cutting the circle

Cutting the tabletop to round has been postponed until now so you could match up the halves perfectly. With the pins and locks installed, you can now mark out the circle and cut it. If you use a rotary cutter such as a router bit, you must climb cut parts of the tabletop so as not to blow out the edge (see "Climb Cutting" on p. 105). To do this, you'll pattern-rout with a handheld plunge router as was done for the expanding racetrack oval table.

1. Start by making a half-circle pattern with a 22-in. radius out of ¾-in. MDF, as shown on p. 94.

2. Position the half-circle pattern on each side of the tabletop, and use a pencil to mark the circle.

3. Using a bandsaw or other saw, cut to within ⅟₁₆ in. of the line.

4. Clamp the pattern to one half of the tabletop, then rout with a flush trimming bit to clean up the waste, climb cutting as needed.

5. Move the pattern around the table 90 degrees at a time, aligning the cut edge with the pattern. Lock the two table halves together so they will support each other and not cause tearout across the break. When you're finished, the two halves of the tabletop should align perfectly.

Cutting the leaves

The leaves should be identical so they can be installed in any order. To make them identical, work on one leaf at a time while the table is standing on its pedestal.

1. Open the tabletop, insert one leaf, and lock it in place. Using a board with a jointed edge as a guide, mark across the leaf from one half of the tabletop to the other.

2. Mark the other end of the leaf, then repeat the procedure for the second and third leaves.

3. Crosscut the leaves to length to within ⅟₁₆ in. of the line.

4. Replace the first leaf in the table and lock it in place, then clamp the jointed board back in place.

5. With a flush trimming bit, rout across the edge, using the board as your pattern. Climb cut the first ¼ in. of the right edge so you don't blow it out, then rout left to right across the remainder. Repeat with all the remaining edges, taking care not to nick the round tabletop.

Edge treatment

The tabletop edge treatment is a half-round profile that echoes the rounded pedestal forms.

1. With the table upside down on your bench, insert all of the leaves and lock the table.

2. Mount a ⅜-in. roundover bit with a bottom bearing in your router.

3. Taking several increasingly deeper passes, rout around the edge of the table, climb cutting in the appropriate places.

Sanding and finishing

1. Remove the leaves, lock the tabletop halves, and sand to 220 grit using a random-orbit sander, making sure the two sides are level.

2. Insert one leaf and sand it level with the two table halves to 220 grit. Don't sand the table halves any more. Hand-sand near the edges if you need to.

3. Remove the first leaf and repeat the process for the second and third leaves.

4. With a 220-grit sanding block, go over every inch of the table looking for any blemishes and dings you may have missed.

5. Finish the table. The original table was finished with hand-rubbed oil and varnish. See appendix 1 on pp. 178–179 for finishing instructions.

QUEEN ANNE TABLE

I have designed this mahogany Queen Anne-inspired table to demonstrate basic veneering. The project focuses on techniques for cutting, jointing, laying up, gluing, and pressing veneer. You will find that using veneer opens up new possibilities for you as a designer, since it frees you to arrange color and grain without having to consider the underlying construction of the piece. Designs that would be difficult or impossible to execute with solid wood become easy in veneer.

If you've worked only in solid wood, veneer may seem mysterious, but it's just wood. It behaves like solid wood. You cut it, glue it, and make parts with it as you do with solid wood.

For a table, the top is the logical place to show off veneer's design possibilities. Not all furniture parts are suitable for veneering, however. The MDF onto which veneer is typically glued is too weak a material for thin legs.

Mass-produced furniture has given veneer a bad name, making it synonymous with inexpensive, shoddy work. In fact, veneered furniture is no better or worse than solid-wood furniture—the quality depends on the level of craftsmanship. Because of the freedom of design that veneer allows, many of the most skilled designers, both historical and modern, have used solid wood and veneer in combination. In this project, I'll show how high-end veneer work is done.

Queen Anne Table

THE TOP OF THE FORMAL VENEERED TABLE is made from MDF covered with book-matched mahogany veneer and edged with solid mahogany. The leg assembly is also made from solid mahogany. Mortise-and-tenon joinery is used to attach the apron to the carved Queen Anne legs with knee blocks. Corner blocks add stability to the structure.

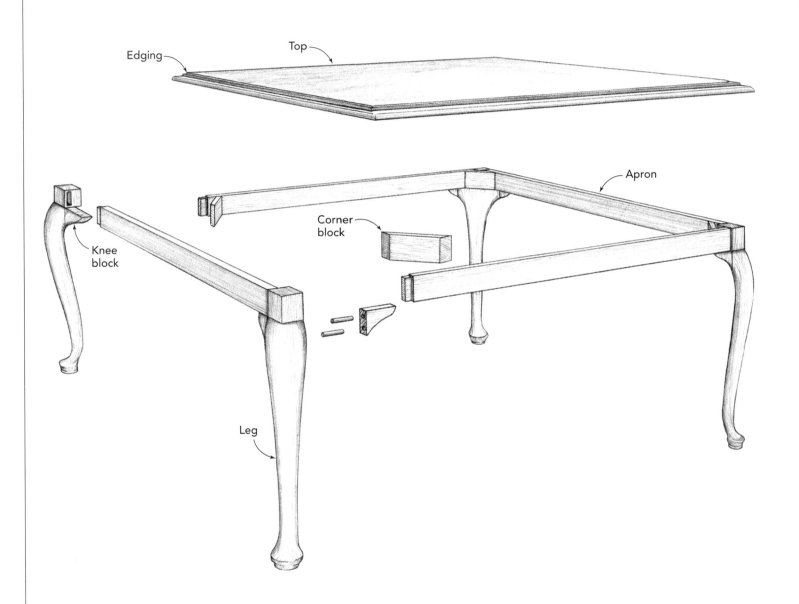

TOP VIEW

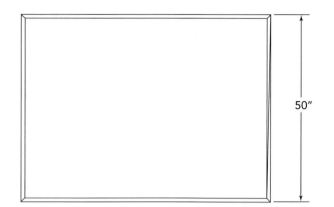

50"

SIDE VIEW

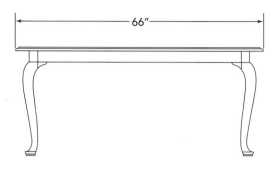

66"

END VIEW

50"

29"

JOINERY DETAILS

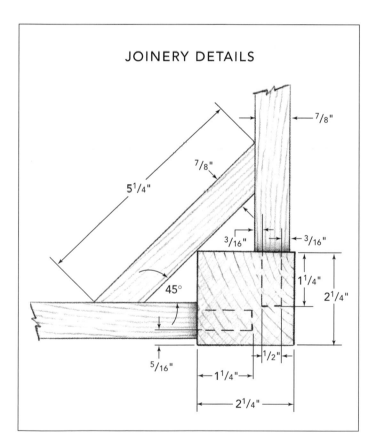

7/8"

5 1/4"

7/8"

3/16"

3/16"

45°

1 1/4"

2 1/4"

5/16"

1/2"

1 1/4"

2 1/4"

LEG AND KNEE BLOCK DIMENSIONS

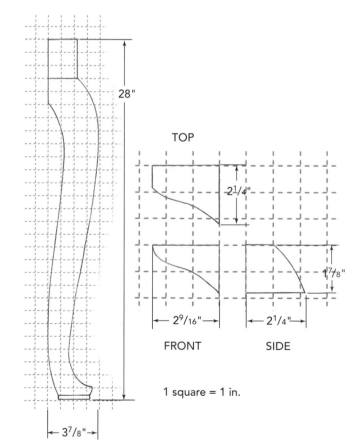

28"

TOP

2 1/4"

1 7/8"

2 9/16"

2 1/4"

FRONT

SIDE

3 7/8"

1 square = 1 in.

BUILDING THE TABLE STEP-BY-STEP

CUT LIST FOR QUEEN ANNE TABLE

Table Parts		
4	Legs	28 in. x 3⅞ in. x 3⅞ in.
2	Long aprons	56¹³⁄₁₆ in. x 3 in. x ⅞ in.
2	Short aprons	40¹³⁄₁₆ in. x 3 in. x ⅞ in.
4	Corner blocks	5¼ in. x 3 in. x ⅞ in.
8	Knee blocks	2⁹⁄₁₆ in. x 1⅞ in. x 2¼ in.
2	Long edging strips	66 in. x 1¹⁄₁₆ in. x 1⅛ in.
2	Short edging strips	50 in. x 1¹⁄₁₆ in. x 1⅛ in.
1	Top panel	64 in. x 48 in. (1-in. MDF)
Veneer		
1	Top veneer	64 in. x 48 in. (mahogany)
1	Bottom veneer	64 in. x 48 in. (mahogany backer veneer)
Materials Used in Construction Process[1]		
1	Veneer jointing jig	4-ft. x 8-ft. sheet of ¾-in. MDF
1	Caul	49 in. x 65 in. (¼-in. melamine)[2]
Other Materials		
14	Tabletop fasteners	
16	Wood screws	#10 x 3 in.
14	Wood screws	#8 x ¾ in.
16	Wooden dowels	⁵⁄₁₆ in. diameter

[1]Other jigs and cauls can be made from scrap.
[2]You may need to glue two pieces of melamine together to make the caul.
Note on veneer: Buy enough leaves so that the narrowest parts of the leaves add up to about 66 in. You need an even number of leaves for the top. The top veneer will be seen and is worth spending money on. Some veneer vendors will send you samples so you can see what you're buying. Mahogany comes in many different species and patterns—ask the vendor how hard a particular species and pattern is to work. For the bottom veneer, you can use backer veneer, the widest, least expensive mahogany in stock.

The joinery for this table has been covered earlier, and the Queen Anne leg is the "alternate leg" shown on p. 77. The top is edge-banded with solid wood to resist the dings of everyday wear and tear. The table seats four for formal service or six informally. If you want to make it into an expanding table, see pp. 88–105 and pp. 106–121 for instructions.

MAKING THE PARTS

Milling the lumber

The critical dimensions for this project are the lengths of the legs and aprons, the thickness of the aprons, and the thickness and width of the legs.

1. Start by milling the solid edging several inches more than finished length so you can adjust your miter if necessary.
2. To mill the legs, crosscut them 1 in. oversize, joint two opposing sides, then plane all four legs to finished dimension and crosscut to finished size.
3. If possible, cut the knee blocks from the same board you cut the legs from so their color will match. The grain in the knee blocks runs vertically, as it does in the leg. You should be able to get all the wood for this table out of one medium-sized 16/4 board, if you can resaw it.
4. Crosscut the aprons 2 in. oversize, along with an additional 24-in. board for corner blocks. Joint two opposing sides of each board, plane them all to finished dimension, and finally crosscut to finished length.

Cutting the joinery

Details of mortise-and-tenon joinery are discussed on pp. 30–34.

1. Measure for the mortise placement and chop the mortises by hand or by using a mortising machine.
2. Measure for the shoulders of the tenons. Using a secondary fence, set a stop on your mortising gauge and cut tenons to match the mortises.
3. Plow rabbets for the tabletop fasteners into the aprons, as described on p. 34.

Making the Queen Anne legs

Although traditional cabriole legs were carved, you can hog out most of the waste using a bandsaw if you make a pattern. The trick is to lay out the pattern properly and follow the correct sequence of cuts.

1. Enlarge the leg illustration shown on p. 125 to full size and glue it to a piece of ¼-in. Masonite or other stiff material. Using a bandsaw or coping saw, cut out the pattern and fair the curves, then trace the pattern onto two adjacent faces of the leg blanks, making sure the knees and feet face each other as shown in **photo A**.

2. Using a ⅛-in. blade and a fence, cut the legs with the bandsaw. Cut the pommel, then the back of the leg and the heel of the foot on one face. Finally, cut the front of the leg from the heel to about ¹⁄₁₆ in. short of the pommel. The waste piece will hinge away from the workpiece, and you can back the blade easily out of the cut. If you break the waste piece off accidentally, reattach it with masking tape or a couple of dots of hot-melt glue (see **photo B**).

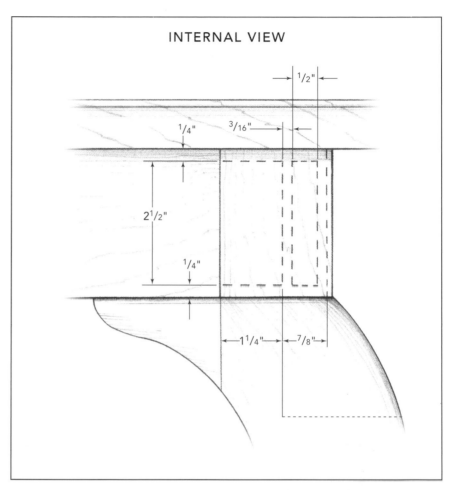

INTERNAL VIEW

Photo A (left): The knees are facing toward each other. Make the straight cuts first, followed by the back of the leg, the foot, and the front of the leg.

Photo B (right): If you don't cut completely through the front, you can use it as a hinge and back out of the cut easily, preserving the pattern for the second set of cuts.

Photo C: The leg
is flat-sided after
you finish bandsaw-
ing it out. Rounding
over the edges gives
it the traditional
curved form.

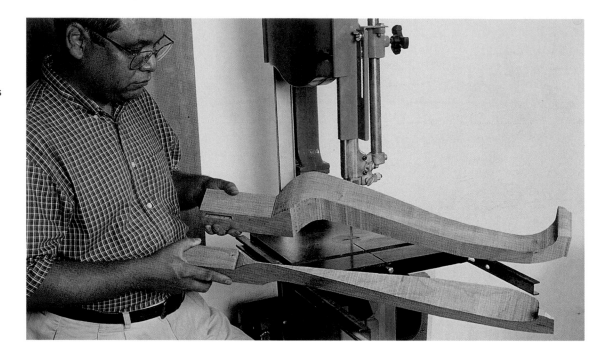

Photo D: Always
carve down the grain.

3. Rotate the workpiece 90 degrees and repeat the cuts in the same order. This time saw through to the pommel, then break off the hinge left from the first cut. Now you have a flat-sided approximation of a rounded cabriole leg (see **photo C**).

4. Clamp the leg to your bench and use a spokeshave or a 1-in. #3 gouge to round over the edges, carving until you get curves you want. Always carve *down* the grain so you won't chip out (see **photo D**). When you first

start to carve, it's hard to know when you've taken off enough wood and it's easy to take off too much. The best advice I can give is to look closely and let the piece tell you when it's done.

5. Next, make the knee blocks. Queen Anne legs should have carved knee blocks that continue the line of the inside of the leg up into the apron. You first need to make three full-sized patterns, using the illustrations shown on p. 125, for the top, front, and side of the blocks.

6. To attach the knee blocks to the legs with two ⁵⁄₁₆-in. dowels, start by marking the positions of the two dowel holes for each block. Set a combination square to ⁵⁄₁₆ in. and draw lines on one side of each block ⁵⁄₁₆ in. from the back, top, and bottom. Where the lines intersect, drill ⁵⁄₁₆-in. dowel holes ⅞ in. deep. Use doweling pins to mark the position of the dowel holes on the legs, and drill those holes as well.

7. Divide the blocks into two sets of four, with the dowel holes of one set facing the dowel holes of the other set. After doing this, the two sets will be mirror images of one another.

8. Trace the three patterns onto the blocks, making sure you have four mirrored pairs of blocks.

9. Bandsaw the parts slightly oversize. Cut the front faces and then the tops, holding the part you're working on with a second part connected to it by dowels (without glue). Finally, cut the sides, holding the parts with a wooden hand screw. Don't completely separate the cutoffs; rather, leave them attached as you did for the legs so you can see the marking lines.

10. When all of the faces are cut, break off the cutoffs, fill the dowel holes with glue, insert the dowels, and glue the knee blocks to the legs.

11. Finish carving the legs and knee blocks with a rasp. Sand the legs to 180 grit.

LAYING UP THE TOP

Making a 48-in.-wide top requires a 5-ft.-wide veneer bag. If you have only a 4-ft. bag, reduce the width of the panel to 46 in. and cut the short aprons 2 in. shorter (38¹³⁄₁₆ in.). The table's proportions will still be fine.

Preparing the substrate and caul

The veneer is laid up, or glued, to an MDF substrate and covered by a melamine caul of the same size. MDF is an ideal substrate because it is stable, very flat, readily available in any commercial lumberyard, and inexpensive. You could lay up veneer onto furniture-grade particleboard or plywood, but don't. MDF is the superior material.

MDF comes about 1 in. over the rated dimensions, so your panels will probably be 49 in. wide. It's easier to lay up veneered panels oversize and cut them to final dimension once the glue has cured, so leave the MDF 49 in. wide, rip the melamine to the same width, and crosscut both of them 1 in. over length.

Preparing the veneer

Veneer leaves are sold in the order in which they are cut from the log. It's important to maintain that order so you can use it as a reference when you're matching the leaves. When you buy a stack of veneer, number the leaves sequentially from 1 to n. Put the numbers in the same position on the sheets so you know not only the order but also the orientation of the leaves (see **photo E**).

Prepare veneer for the top and bottom of the tabletop. Veneering the underside of the table may seem odd, but a balanced panel needs veneer on both sides (see p. 99). Using the same species for top and bottom looks bet-

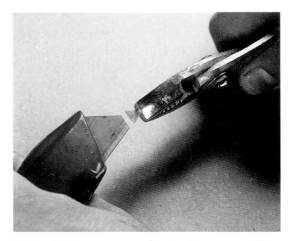

Photo F: You can get a fresh edge on a utility knife blade by grasping the tip with a pair of pliers and snapping the tip off. Use eye protection for this operation.

Photo G: Holding one end of the masking tape down, pull it taut and stretch it across the joint. Don't pull too tight or the joint won't lie flat. A tape dispenser is helpful.

Tip: If you veneer one side of a panel, always veneer the other side to create a balanced panel that will stay flat.

ter, but it isn't necessary to use the same cut. For the bottom of this table, you can buy wide, inexpensive sheets of mahogany called mahogany backer veneer.

Cutting the veneer to length

1. If necessary, trim the ends of all the leaves so they're nice and neat.
2. Cut the veneer to length 1 in. oversize, using the mat knife technique shown on pp. 92–93 (see **photo F**).

Jointing the veneer

Using the jig shown on p. 132, joint the veneer. The sheet of veneer should be slightly wider than the length of the substrate—in this case, 64 in. Therefore, the finished width of each leaf must equal the width of the substrate divided by the number of leaves. For example, if you're using six leaves on this table, each leaf should be a little more than one-sixth of 64 in., or $10^{11}/_{16}$ in. wide.

Matching and taping the veneer

The artistry of veneer work lies in choosing the right veneer and matching it beautifully. For this table, you will slip-match the bottom backer veneer and book-match the top (see "Matching Veneer" on p. 134). Pay close attention to what these two matches look like as you do them. Once you know what the patterns look like, mistakes become apparent immediately.

1. To slip-match the bottom of the panel, place the cut panel of MDF on your workbench so you have enough space to work. Untape the book of backer veneer, pulling the tape toward the edge so you don't break off the edges. Keeping the leaves in order and oriented in the same direction, place them side by side across the panel.
2. Turn all of the leaves wrong side up and tape them with masking tape. Because masking tape stretches, this draws the seams together tightly (see **photo G**).
3. Turn the sheet over again and tape the seams together with veneer tape, as shown in **photo H**. Veneer tape is a very thin tape coated

Photo H: Tape down the seams on the right side of the veneer, using an envelope moistener to wet the tape. Flatten any irregularities with a hard rubber or steel roller.

Photo I: This finished sheet is ready for pressing. The veneer tape faces out, and the masking tape has been removed from the bottom.

with a water-based glue (see Sources of Supply on p. 183).

4. When the veneer tape is dry, turn the sheet over again and remove the masking tape, as shown in **photo I**.

5. To book-match the top, untape the stack of top veneer and book-match the leaves across the panel. Once you decide on a sequence,

tape the leaves together, following the same sequence of steps as for the bottom veneer.

Gluing up the panel

If you're experienced with veneering, you can press the bottom and top veneer at the same time, using a second caul between the bottom veneer and the platen. But if you're trying it

Tip: Always remove the masking tape from veneer before gluing, or its outline will telegraph through the veneer.

VENEER JOINTING JIG

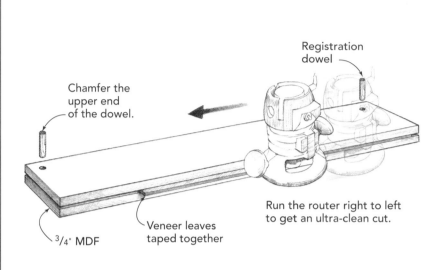

Chamfer the upper end of the dowel.

Registration dowel

Run the router right to left to get an ultra-clean cut.

Veneer leaves taped together

3/4" MDF

To make this jig, cut two pieces of ¾-in. MDF 18 in. wide by 8 ft. long and screw them together with drywall screws. Drill two 1-in. holes through both layers. Unscrew the layers and glue two 1-in.-diameter by 2-in. dowels into the bottom layer, first chamfering the upper ends of the dowels so the upper layer will register easily. When the glue is dry, put the top layer over the registration pegs and run the entire jig through the table saw, ripping the long registration edge of both layers so the top and bottom are perfectly aligned.

To get a good edge on the veneer, use a sharp bit and climb cut the stack from right to left. Adjust the clamps as needed to get good pressure on the stack.

Veneer must be jointed so the edges of the leaves match perfectly, or you'll see gaps when you glue them to the substrate. You should joint the whole stack of leaves (I call it a book) at the same time. To do this, tape the book together with masking tape, then tape it to the lower level of the jig. Put the top on and clamp it in place. Use a ½-in.-diameter flush trimming bit with a ½-in. shank (Amana makes a three-fluted bit, which is ideal; save it just for veneer). With your router speed set to maximum, rout from right to left, climb cutting the stack. If necessary, use a sanding block with 220-grit paper to clean up the last whiskers of waste. Sand very lightly so as not to ruin the reference edge of the jig.

When one side is jointed, take the book out of the jig. Using a combination square and pencil, mark the finished width of the veneer on the lower level of the jig. Mark it in two or more places, then match the jointed edge to your pencil marks and tape the book down with masking tape. Put on the top layer of the jig, reclamp, and joint the second edge with your router.

for the first time, practice on the bottom first to learn how much glue is needed.

1. To glue up the panel, use the melamine caul you cut earlier. (I've used melamine because glue doesn't stick to it.) Round over the top edges and corners with a mill file so the sharp edges won't pierce the bag when it's placed under pressure (see **photo J**). Set up the vacuum pressing system, and position the substrate and veneer so they can be slipped easily into the bag.

2. Wearing your protective gear, mix up the urea resin. Pour the glue onto the substrate, and roll it out with a short-napped paint roller or, even better, a roller especially made for glue. Cover the entire surface until it is wet but not runny.

3. Place the backer veneer over the substrate with the veneer tape facing up, and align the veneer so the seams run parallel to the short edges of the substrate. (Make sure you have removed the masking tape from the underside.) If necessary, tape the veneer to the substrate with masking tape so it won't shift when you move the assembly into the bag.

Photo J: The veneer bag is easily punctured. You can make it last longer by not storing things on it, by checking the platen for dried glue, and by rounding over the corners of your cauls.

4. Place the caul over the veneer and slip the assembly into the veneer press, then close the bag and turn on the pump. Hold the corners down so you get a good seal around the edges (see **photo K**).

5. Put some extra glue into a plastic bag or wrap it in waxed paper and put it on top of the bag. When the glue is hard, take the panel out of the bag and look at it. If you used too much glue, you'll see bleed-through; if you

Photo K: This is a big, awkward, and heavy assembly. You might need a second pair of hands to help spread glue, put the workpiece into the bag, and hold the other two corners tight as the bag deflates.

MATCHING VENEER

Imagine two leaves of veneer, one on top of the other, with pages A, B, C, and D, top to bottom.

If you open the two leaves as you would a book, exposing pages B and C, you have a book-match. Because adjoining leaves have matched grain, page B is a mirror image of page C. Opening the top leaf to the right (imagining the book binding is on the right) gives you a very different book-matched figure. Flipping the two leaves over so page D is next to page A gives you yet another book-match, but a subtly different one—even though veneer is very thin, the grain changes as you go through the flitch.

Obviously, a book-match always has an even number of leaves, or the match won't be symmetrical. Buy an even number of leaves and adjust the width to fit your panel when you joint the veneer.

To create a book-match with four, six, or more leaves, open the "book" like an accordion. Whatever the number of leaves, there are still only four workable arrangements to choose among. You can tape the edges as shown in the illustration at right to create the two possible "accordion" sequences. Try both and decide which has the more interesting and dramatic figure. Then flip over the accordion you've chosen and make the choice between the two subtly different sides.

Returning to the two-leaf example, flipping the first leaf up so the top of page B abuts the top of page C gives a book-and-butt match. This is similar to a book-match but is mirrored along the horizontal rather than the vertical axis.

Slip-matching involves taking our hypothetical stack of veneer and moving the top leaf to the right so page A is next to page C. This repeats the patterns in the veneer rather than mirroring them. Again, you could turn both leaves over so page B is next to page D, or slip the top leaf to the left instead of the right.

By using these three basic strategies and cutting the veneer in various shapes, you can create dozens of patterns (see Further Reading on p. 184 for references to books on veneer patterns).

VENEER MATCHING

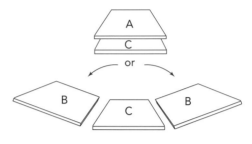

BOOK-MATCH

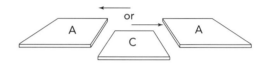

SLIP-MATCH

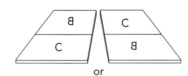

BOOK-AND-BUTT MATCH

In a book-match you open the first leaf either to the left or to the right. For a slip-match, slip the first leaf either left or right. For a book-and-butt-match, open the first leaf either to the top or the bottom.

BOOK-MATCHING MULTIPLE LEAVES

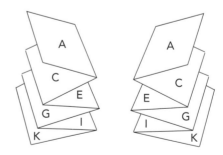

To create a book-match of multiple leaves, open the flitch like an accordion either left or right. These two permutations give very different results because they mirror different parts of the grain pattern.

GLUING VENEER

Two kinds of glue are used in modern veneering: PVA and two-part urea resin. Because urea resin cures to a hard state while PVA cures to a semi-hard state, some people prefer to use urea resin for all veneer applications. However, since PVA is easier to use, less expensive, and nontoxic, I prefer to use it where indicated. Here's a rule I learned from Darryl Keil, president of Vacuum Pressing Systems, about which glue to use:

If you can answer "yes" to any of the following questions, use urea resin. If all the answers are "no," you can use PVA.

- Are you veneering the top of a horizontal surface? (Horizontal surfaces, especially tabletops, get more wear than vertical surfaces, and urea resin makes a rigid glueline.)
- Have you used more than one species of wood in combination for the lay-up?
- Have some pieces of veneer been rotated relative to others, as in marquetry or parquetry applications?
- Is the veneer a burl, crotch, or other highly figured wood?
- Do you need a long open time for the glue-up?

Applying the rule, you must use urea resin for the tabletop of the Queen Anne table, and in order to maintain a balanced panel you must use the same glue on the underside. For basic instructions on using urea resin glue, see "Glue for Laminations" on p. 100.

Spread glue only onto the substrate, not the veneer, being sure to spread it evenly with a paint roller. Use just enough glue so you don't get dry spots. If you put on too much, remove the excess with an old plastic credit card. If you use too much glue, it will be drawn through the veneer and show, or bleed through, onto the surface. It is difficult to fix bleed-through without a great deal of work. And if you sand or scrape through the veneer trying to fix the bleed-through, you can ruin the panel and have to patch, start over, or use fancy finishing techniques to hide the flaw.

The balance between too much and too little is delicate. You learn by experience. Since you're practicing on the underside first, err on the side of too much and then decrease if necessary on the top.

didn't use enough, you'll have loose spots. Don't worry; it's the underside of the table, but note any problems. File off any sharp glue on the edges so you don't puncture the bag when you press the top.

6. Turn the panel over and repeat the process for the top, adjusting the amount of glue to account for any problems you found.

7. Once the glue has cured, take the panel out of the press and let it sit overnight in a warm place to cure before you trim it.

VACUUM PRESSING

The vacuum press has revolutionized veneer work, replacing complex positive and negative cauls, hundreds of clamps, screw presses, and hammer veneering techniques. It is suitable not only for flat surfaces but also for curved panels, bent laminations, and torsion boxes. You can make your own vacuum press or buy a press such as the one shown in the photo below from a commercial supplier (see Sources of Supply on p. 183).

The vacuum press is a large plastic bag connected by a hose to a vacuum pump, which draws air out of the bag once it is sealed. The workpiece typically rests on a melamine platen. Another piece of melamine is placed on top of the workpiece as a caul. The bag is sealed, the pump turned on, and air withdrawn. Once a vacuum is created, atmospheric pressure presses down on the bag with a force of about 12 pounds per square inch, creating a very even and effective clamp. In addition, the vacuum draws the air out of the cells of the wood, allowing the glue to penetrate it. For more information about presses, see *The Veneering Book* by David Shath Square (The Taunton Press, 1995).

Commercial presses like this one from Vacuum Pressing Systems have automatic valves that regulate pressure without running the motor continuously. The regulator cuts down on the noise and limits wear on the motor.

FINISHING THE PANEL

Cutting to size

It's difficult to get a clean crosscut on a veneered panel without the right technique and sawblades. Luckily, no one will see the bottom of the table, so only the top has to be perfect.

1. Mount a sharp, high-quality crosscut blade with at least 60 teeth in your table saw so you can cut the panel in one pass rather than having to score it first. (If possible, use a Hi-A/T blade especially made for veneered sheet goods—see Sources of Supply on p. 183.) Raise the blade to $\frac{1}{16}$ in. above the surface of the tabletop.

SEQUENCE FOR MITERING

Cut and glue in the first piece.

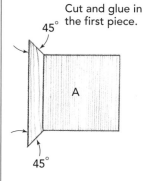

Microadjust this angle to fit the miter.

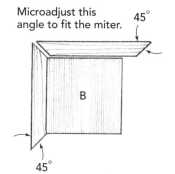

Cut the molding to length using the same setting.

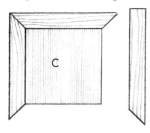

Repeat the sequence going around the panel.

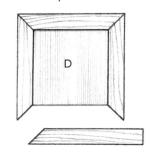

Microadjust both miters of the last piece.

Miter saws are rarely adjusted perfectly, and panels are seldom perfectly square. In order to get tight miters, follow this sequence. Remember that once you've cut the edging it is no longer symmetrical, so mark the proper position of each piece as you go.

EDGE TREATMENT

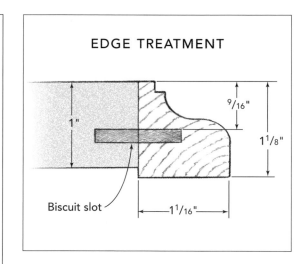

Biscuit slot

2. With the panel right side up, set a stop on your miter gauge and crosscut, scoring the underside.

3. Raise the blade so the teeth just clear the panel, and run the panel back through the table saw, crosscutting it to establish a reference edge.

4. Drop the blade back so it is just above the surface, and reset your stop to final length. Reverse your panel and score the underside of the other end of the panel, then raise the blade and cut the panel to final length.

5. Finally, rip the panel to width, making sure to keep the middle joint and the panel figure centered on the panel. When you're ripping you shouldn't have to score the underside. Rip one edge to establish a reference edge, then reverse the panel and rip it to final width.

Adding the solid-wood edging

The edging is mitered, then glued to the panel using biscuits for alignment. After it is attached, the edge treatment is cut.

1. Lay the panel on a clean surface, top side up.
2. On one end of one piece of edging, cut a 45-degree miter.

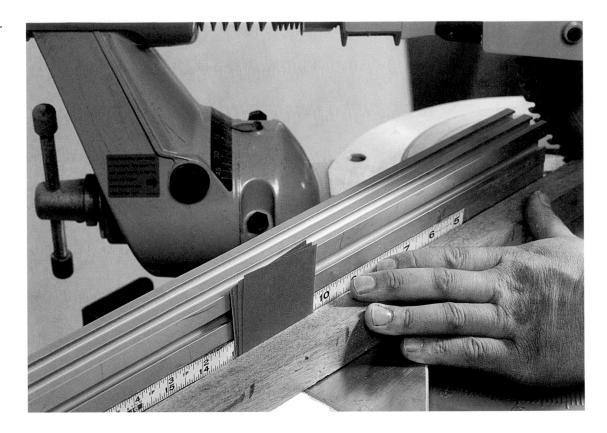

3. Mark the edging strip for length and cut the second end. You'll want to sneak up on the exact length. Make it right on.

4. Set the biscuit jointer so the slot is below the halfway point of the edging, as shown in the illustration at right on p. 137. You don't want to hit the slot when cutting the edge treatment later.

5. Mark the edging for biscuit slots and cut the slots.

6. Next, place a piece of 180-grit sandpaper between the fence and the tabletop and rout the slots in the table edge. The sandpaper raises the slots slightly, which raises the level of the edging. This allows you to sand the edging flush with the tabletop without going through the veneer.

7. Glue the first piece of edging to the tabletop.

8. Cut a 45-degree miter on the second piece of edging. You might need to microadjust the miter with paper shims for the second miter.

Cut it to length and glue it in place (see **photo L**).

9. Repeat the process for the third edging piece.

10. For the last piece of edging, you will have to microadjust both miters and then cut the piece to length. Although this sequence seems time-consuming, it is actually the fastest way to get all the miters correct the first time.

Cutting the edge treatment

1. Mount the router bit into your router. Since this is a large cut, use a bit with a ½-in. shank and a large router with adjustable speeds.

2. Clamp the panel to your bench, protecting the surface with a clamp block.

3. Taking progressively deeper cuts, hog out the waste, routing left to right. The finishing cuts should be very shallow (½₂ in. or less) and should be climb cut right to left to assure a clean surface. Adjust the router speed so that it's slow enough not to burn the work but high enough to get a clean cut.

Photo M: Wetting and scraping the veneer tape is preferable to sanding it off, since it reduces the risk of sanding through the veneer.

ASSEMBLING AND FINISHING UP

Sanding

1. Using a sponge, wet the veneer tape thoroughly and let it soak for several minutes. You may need to do this several times until the glue lets go. Then take a cabinet scraper and gently scrape off the tape. It should come off in one swipe (see **photo M**).

2. Sand the legs and aprons to 180 grit.

3. Sand the edging level to the veneered panel with 150-grit paper on a random-orbit sander.

4. Switching to 180-grit paper, sand the veneer until it's smooth and level, then stop. If you go through the veneer, you're in big trouble—practice on the underside of the table if this is your first time. Make sure you take off all the glue left from the veneer tape.

Assembly

The table is assembled in the same way as the kitchen table on pp. 37–39. Assemble the legs and aprons, screw on the corner blocks, and attach the top with tabletop fasteners. Finally, go over every part of the table with a sanding block, looking for any flaws you might have missed.

Finishing

The best way to finish this table is to spray it with a couple of coats of orange shellac for color and then finish it with enough coats of lacquer to give a thick, rich coat. However, if you don't have spray equipment, several coats of gel-varnish will give a nice, hard top coat.

Modern Round Table

Sometimes it takes a challenge to inspire a creative and elegant solution. Kirk Schuly, the owner of KS Furniture and Design in New York City, needed a table for his Manhattan apartment. Kirk and his girlfriend Jackie like to cook and entertain, but like most New Yorkers, they have very little space. An expanding table wouldn't do them much good.

Kirk also wanted to use four armchairs he had already built, and, again because of space limitations, he needed to fit them under the table when they weren't in use. In this table, which seats four if he serves from the kitchen counter, he's substituted cross braces for the usual apron. This puts the braces out of the way of the chair arms but still allows them to support the top and control racking forces.

Kirk designed the tabletop to demonstrate more of veneer's many possibilities. The tabletop is laid up in a traditional reverse-diamond pattern with an inlay added between the veneer and the solid-wood edge. In this project, I'll look at veneer matching in more depth than I did in the last one. I'll also introduce two new techniques: making inlays and making negative patterns.

As usual, you are encouraged to modify the design to your own tastes. Changing the veneer and the match would radically alter the look of the table, as would modifying the shape of the legs.

Modern Round Table

THE MODERN ROUND TABLE uses stretcher-type construction rather than aprons. Cross braces that connect the opposing turned legs are joined to them with floating tenons. A lap joint is used where the two braces cross. The leg assembly is screwed to a subtop, which in turn is screwed to the underside of the tabletop.

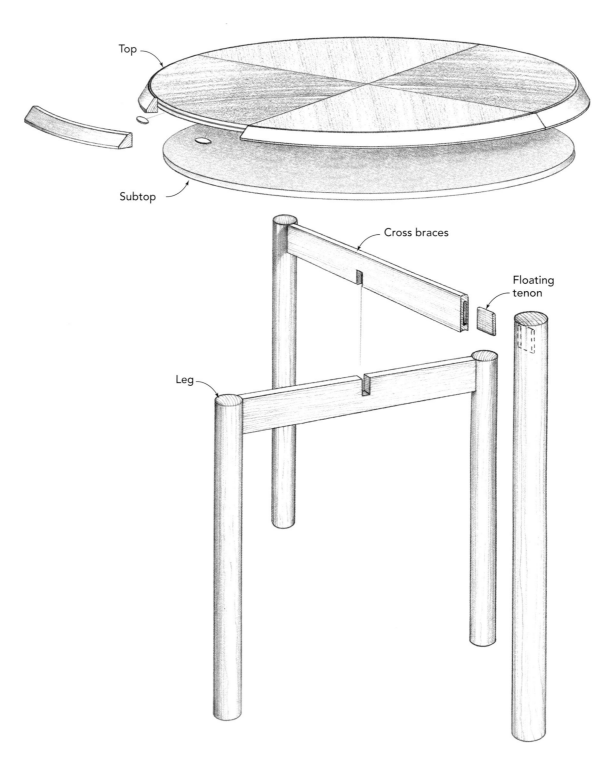

Top

Subtop

Cross braces

Floating tenon

Leg

TOP VIEW

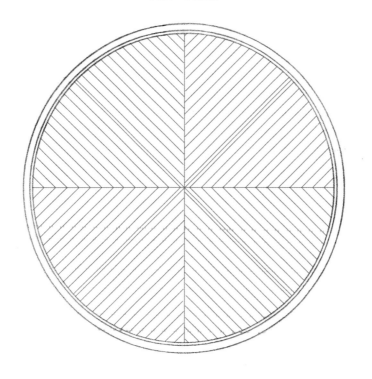

FLOATING TENON DETAIL

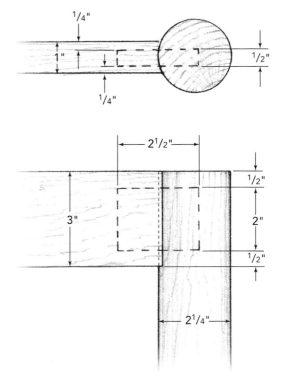

1/4"

1"

1/4"

1/2"

2 1/2"

1/2"

3"

2"

1/2"

2 1/4"

FRONT VIEW

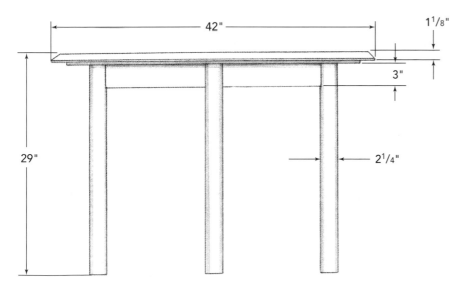

42"

1 1/8"

3"

29"

2 1/4"

EDGE TREATMENT DETAIL

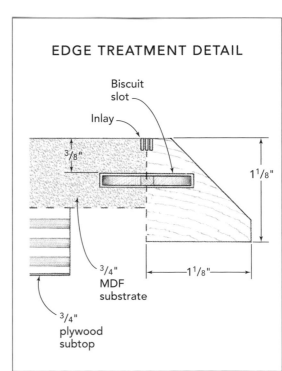

Biscuit slot

Inlay

3/8"

1 1/8"

3/4"
MDF
substrate

1 1/8"

3/4"
plywood
subtop

BUILDING THE TABLE STEP-BY-STEP

CUT LIST FOR MODERN ROUND TABLE

Table Parts

4	Legs	27½ in. x 2¼ in. x 2¼ in.
2	Cross braces	28 in. x 3 in. x 1 in.
8	Edging strips	17¹¹⁄₁₆ in. x 3 in. x 1⅛ in.
1	Tabletop	40 in. x 40 in. (¾-in. MDF)
1	Subtop	38 in. x 38 in. (¾-in. birch plywood)
4	Floating tenons	2½ in. x 1¾ in. x ½ in.

Veneer

1	Top veneer	Quartersawn sapele
1	Backer veneer	Mahogany
5	Inlay	36 in. x 3 in. 2 black (dyed), 2 white (holly), and 1 dark mahogany

Other Materials

4	Steel wood screws	#8 x 1 in.
8	Steel wood screws	#8 x 2 in.
8	Steel wood screws	#8 x 1¼ in.
8	Biscuits	#20
	Mahogany edgebanding	11 ft.

This small table, with its deceptively simple, modern lines, probably offers more challenges per square inch than any other table in this book. When you pull off all the miters—and the veneer meets at sharp points in the center of the table—you'll know you've really done a good job.

You'll make the legs and cross braces first. The legs are turned, and floating tenons connect them to the cross braces. A lap joint is used where the two cross braces meet. The tabletop is the more difficult part of the table and requires careful measurement and attention. You'll lay up the veneer first, then add the round edging, and finally make and install the inlay between the veneer and edging. If these techniques are new to you—or even if they aren't—you'll find that working systematically is the fastest and easiest way to finish the table.

MAKING THE PARTS

Milling the stock

The only critical dimensions are the length and diameter of the legs. The shoulders joining the cross braces to the legs are curved to fit over the round legs. Because of the way the curved shoulders are cut, the diameter of the legs must be consistent. The leg can be a little wide, but it can't be small or the shoulders won't be tight.

1. Cut the legs from 10/4 stock, and dimension them square so you can center the mortise accurately. Set a stop and cut the four legs to length.
2. Mill the cross braces 6 in. more than the final length. You'll need the extra length to make the curved shoulders.
3. For the top, cut the ¾-in. MDF several inches oversize and leave it square. You'll lay up the veneer onto the square top and then cut the circle.
4. Cut the edging several inches long so you have enough stock to adjust your miters.

Making the legs

1. Mark for and cut ½-in. mortises on the leg blanks, centering them accurately between the edges (see **photo A**). For floating tenon joints, I recommend milling the mortises in both

parts with a horizontal mortiser because it's fast and safe. However, if you don't have a horizontal mortiser, you can use a standard mortising machine as shown on p. 31 to cut the mortises in the legs and a doweling jig for the mortises in the cross braces. This method is slower and not as accurate, but since there are only eight mortises to cut it shouldn't be a problem.

2. Mill the legs to diameter. Duplicating the legs, with their long straight lines, can be difficult unless you have access to a spindle-duplicating machine. If you're duplicating by hand, hold a long steel rule against the spinning work. The burnish marks will show you where the high and low spots are. If you need to err, make the diameter slightly large rather than too small. When you get close to the finished diameter, use the steel rule, then 80-grit sandpaper to take down the high spots. Sand the legs on the lathe to 150 grit (see **photo B**).

Photo B: Although you can turn the legs by hand, the duplicator excels at long straights or gentle curves. The microadjust allows you to turn very accurate diameters.

JOINERY OPERATIONS

Making the lap joints

Make the lap joints in the cross braces first, then cut the shoulders.

1. Mount a dado set on the table saw, and raise the dado to half the width of the cross braces.

2. Mark the centers of the cross braces, then set a stop on the miter gauge and cut through the center of one brace. Reverse the workpiece and cut again so the slot is exactly centered.

3. Repeat with the second brace.

4. Adjust the stop and continue making cuts until one brace just fits over the other.

Making the shoulders

The curved shoulder is cut using a 2¼-in. Forstner bit in a drill press. Assuming the legs have a diameter of 2¼ in., the shoulder should fit perfectly. If the leg diameter is less than 2¼ in., adjust the size of the Forstner bit accordingly. For the shoulder to fit tightly, the bit diameter must be the same as or slightly smaller than the leg diameter.

1. Using a marking gauge, find the middle of one end of the cross brace, and prick the point with an awl.

2. Mount the Forstner bit in the drill press.

3. Position the workpiece and clamp a fence to your drill-press table to hold that position.

4. Clamp the brace and cut the shoulder on one end (see **photo C**). Repeat with the other brace.

5. Next, set a stop on the fence and cut the other two ends, adjusting the stop to get the correct length.

Making the floating tenon joints

Use the horizontal mortising machine with the same bit you used on the legs to mill the mortises in the cross braces.

1. Position the workpiece on the table and set the stops.

2. Take several shallow passes into the end grain until you reach the full depth of the mortise. Repeat for the remaining three mortises.

3. Plane the spline board until it just fits into the mortise in the cross brace. Rout the tops and bottoms of the sides with a ¼-in. round-over bit so it will fit the curved mortise sides created by the horizontal mortiser.

4. Cut the four splines to length and test-fit them in the mortises. If necessary, sand, file, or plane to final fit.

Photo C: A Forstner bit gives you a clean shoulder on which to register the leg.

> **Tip:** *You'll need an 8-in. dado set to make the lap joints. If yours is smaller, use a regular sawblade, then waste the area in the middle with multiple passes.*

VENEERING THE TABLETOP

To make the tabletop, you'll lay up and press the veneer onto the top and bottom of the substrate, then cut the table to round. You'll make a negative pattern from the tabletop and use it to cut the inside of the edging. You'll then miter, attach, and cut the edging to round. Finally, you'll install an inlay between the veneer and the edging and cut the edge treatment.

Laying up and pressing the backer veneer

1. Lay up the backer veneer as discussed on pp. 129–131.
2. Press the veneer onto the substrate using urea resin, and let the glue cure overnight.

Making the reverse-diamond pattern

There's more to veneering than matching up the grain patterns. In a complex design such as the reverse diamond, you must also take "pattern jump" and light refraction into account.

Pattern jump is the variation between sequential leaves of veneer. Even though veneer is very thin, the pattern you see on the first leaf will change as you go through the flitch until it won't look at all like the first. Since the veneered surface is most attractive when adjacent leaves are similar looking, it's best to minimize pattern jump.

When you're laying out four or more leaves around a table, don't lay them out sequentially, which places the first leaf next to the last (see example 1 in the top left illustration on p. 148). Your best strategy is alternating them, as shown in example 2. If your veneer isn't wide enough to use one leaf per segment, you can slip-match up to four leaves for each segment as shown in example 3. This creates more of a pattern jump than in example 2, but with the straight-grained veneer that you use in diamond and reverse-diamond patterns, the pattern jump is still acceptable.

FLOATING TENON JOINTS

A floating (or loose) tenon joint is a form of a mortise and tenon where a separate tenon fits into two mortises, as shown in the illustration below. This joint can be even stronger than a standard mortise-and-tenon joint because the grain direction in the spline is always long grain. You'll use it in this table because it makes it easier to mill the curved shoulders of the cross braces. This kind of joint is very useful in chairmaking.

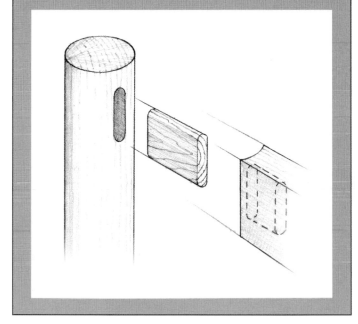

Tip: *If you do not have a horizontal mortiser, you can use a self-centering doweling jig with a ½-in. brad-point bit to mill the mortises into the ends of the cross braces. Cut four or more overlapping holes, then chisel out the waste.*

MINIMIZING PATTERN JUMP

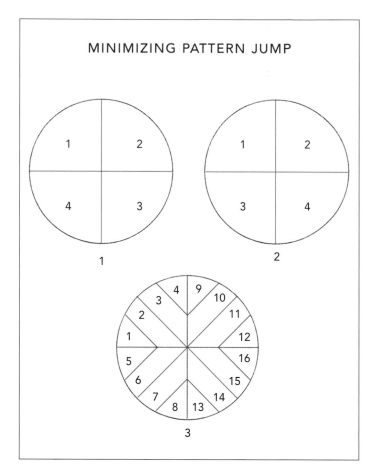

SLIP-MATCHING AND REFRACTION

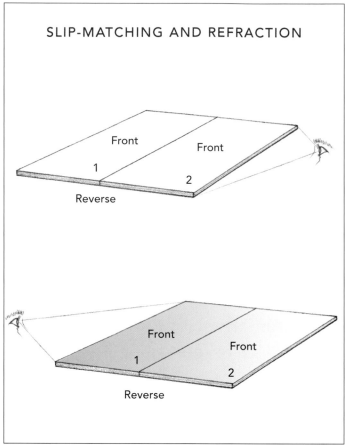

MATCHING REFRACTION PATTERNS

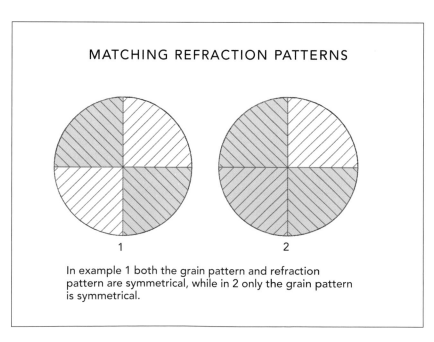

In example 1 both the grain pattern and refraction pattern are symmetrical, while in 2 only the grain pattern is symmetrical.

Refraction is a trickier issue. Veneer can look either dark or shiny, depending on how light falls on it (think of the patterns made on a baseball field by the grounds crew). The difference is caused by refraction of light against the surface. Just as you maintain the grain pattern in a match, you should also create a dark/shiny pattern that makes sense.

Slip-matching and book-matching don't pose refraction problems. If you slip-match two pieces of veneer, they're oriented the same way, so both pieces of veneer look either shiny or dull from the same position. Slip-matching quartersawn or other straight-grained veneer makes what looks like one large sheet. In a book-match, the adjacent pieces are symmetrical not only in pattern but also in their refraction of light.

In diamond and reverse-diamond matches, however, you need to be more careful to preserve the orientation of the leaves so you

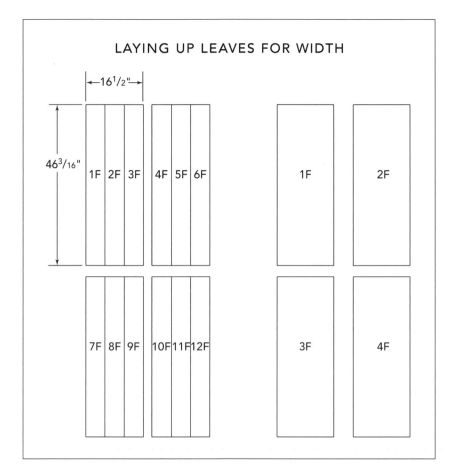

LAYING UP LEAVES FOR WIDTH

←16¹/₂"→

46³/₁₆"

1F | 2F | 3F   4F | 5F | 6F

1F

2F

7F | 8F | 9F   10F|11F|12F

3F

4F

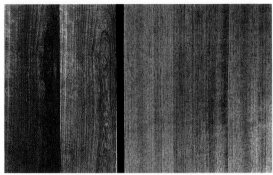

Photo D: Slip-matching with straight-grained material like quartersawn sapele (left) gives the effect of one wide leaf. Slip-matching with nonquartersawn figure (the cherry on the right) doesn't work because the figure repeats.

don't get results like those shown in 2 of the bottom illustration on the facing page. That makes these matches far more complicated to execute.

You'll make a diamond match first, then use it to create a reverse diamond. I recommend practicing with pieces of paper before trying to make up the match with the veneer.

The diamond match is made from four leaves of straight-grained veneer. Quartersawn sapele is good because it has straight lines and no figure, but it doesn't come in leaves wide enough to make up the match you need. You'll need to slip-match two, three, or four leaves together, as shown in the illustration above, to make sheets 16½ in. wide and 46³⁄₁₆ in. long. (This means you'll need 8, 12, or 16 sequential leaves in all.)

1. Cut the sequential leaves to length, then joint the veneer to width. Lay it up into four

sheets. Renumber the sheets on their smooth front sides from 1F to 4F and on their rough back sides from 1R to 4R (see **photo D**). Stack the four renumbered leaves together, front side up and oriented the same way (check for orientation by making sure they all look dark or shiny from the same position), and tape them together. Rejoint them so they're all identical. Carefully measure out 45-degree triangles on both ends of the stack, and cut off the triangles using the routing jig shown on p. 132, leaving four rhomboids as shown in the illustration on p. 150.

2. Pick up leaves 1 and 2 and open leaf 2 to the right from underneath so that the tops of 1F and 2R abut. Temporarily tape the top edges together with masking tape (A). Repeat the process with leaves 3 and 4, but this time open leaf 3 to the right from above so that 4F is to the left of 3R (B).

Creating the Reverse Diamond

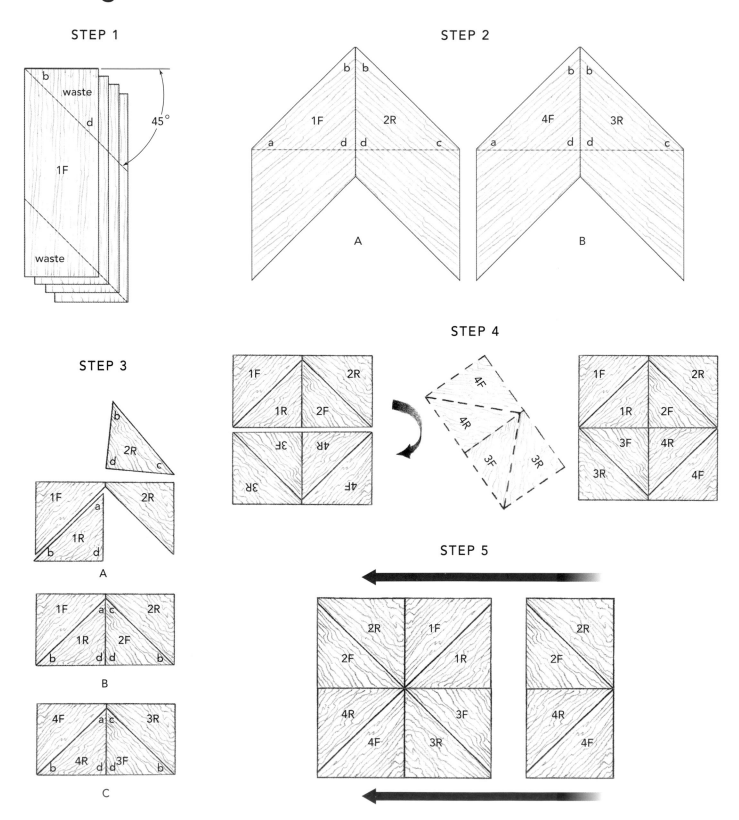

STEP 1

STEP 2

STEP 3

STEP 4

STEP 5

Photo E: A reverse diamond is ready for pressing. Note that the dark and light refraction squares are opposite each other. Line the edges with veneer tape to keep the veneer from tearing as you handle it.

3. Next, rough-cut across line ac of both pieces with a straightedge and sharp mat knife. Be careful when cutting across the jointed edge (bd) and when exiting at point c. Carefully remove the tape holding the top edges together. Flip half of the left-hand sheet, then half of the right-hand sheet, creating the arrangements shown (B, C).

4. To create the diamond pattern, rotate leaves 3 and 4 180 degrees and abut them with leaves 1 and 2. As you can see, this method preserves the pattern and the pattern jump. What you can't see in the illustration is that the refraction pattern is preserved as well.

5. To transform the diamond pattern to a reverse-diamond pattern, simply slip the right half across to the left. The bottom illustration on the facing page shows the resulting symmetry.

6. Turn the whole figure over and pull the edges tight with masking tape. Match up all the points in the center, then tape that as well. Turn the lay-up over to the right side, and tape all the seams with veneer tape (see **photo E**). When the veneer tape is dry, remove the masking tape from the wrong side.

7. Press the veneer onto the substrate using urea resin, and let the glue cure overnight.

ROUTING A NEGATIVE CURVE

You can make a negative pattern for any curved edge by making a positive interim pattern and then making the negative pattern from it. The method shown here works for any curve a 1-in. bushing can follow.

Start by fitting a ½-in. O.D. bushing onto your router base and mounting a ¼-in. bit in it. Attach a piece of MDF larger than the tabletop to its underside. Run the bushing against the tabletop to cut through the MDF, and make a positive interim pattern with a radius slightly larger than the original tabletop. Next, attach the interim pattern to another sheet of MDF, and mount a 1-in. O.D. bushing onto your router base. Using the same 1/4-in. bit you used before, run the 1-in. bushing against the edge of the interim pattern to make the negative—a sheet of MDF with a hole in it the size of your original tabletop.

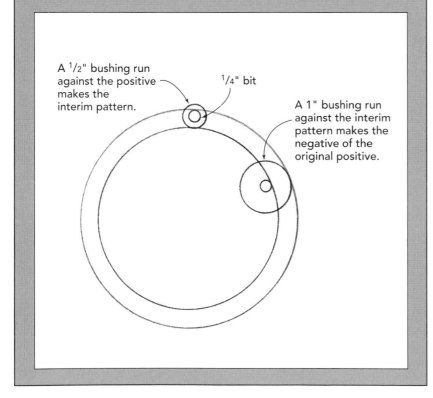

A ¹/₂" bushing run against the positive makes the interim pattern.

¹/₄" bit

A 1" bushing run against the interim pattern makes the negative of the original positive.

Photo F: This method for making a negative pattern works equally well with any curve that can be followed by a 1-in. bushing, not just a circle.

FINISHING THE TOP

The center of the table is where the veneer meets in the center of the pattern, whether or not this is the center of the panel.

1. Cut a 6-in. by 6-in. piece of scrap sheet goods square, and mark across the diagonals to find its center. Put a sixpenny finishing nail through the center.

2. Position the scrap on the tabletop with the nail facing up, and center it by aligning its corners with the gluelines on the tabletop. Secure it with double-faced tape. Place another piece of scrap under the tabletop.

3. Using a pivot with the finishing nail as the center and a downward-cutting spiral bit, rout

Photo G: It's worth the time to make a jig using the negative edge; you'll get much more consistent results. Glue and screw the stops in place, then screw the toggle clamps down with drywall screws.

the circle in several passes. Don't remove the pivot when you're done.

4. Cut the subtop to dimension, using the same router jig and another pivot.

Making the negative pattern

1. Secure a 2-ft. by 2-ft. sheet of ½-in. MDF to the underside of the tabletop, and make a one-quarter interim pattern using the method shown in the sidebar on the facing page.

2. Using the interim pattern, cut a one-quarter negative pattern. When it's finished, the negative should fit perfectly against the edge of the tabletop, as shown in **photo F**.

Cutting the edging

1. Position one of the edging strips on the negative pattern so its two front corners touch the curve. Use a pencil to trace the curve on the edging strip, and bandsaw out the shape to within ¹⁄₁₆ in. of the line. Remember that the waste is what's inside the circle, and you're keeping the part outside the circle.

2. Make the pattern into a jig by positioning stops on it to register the workpiece and using fast-action toggle clamps to hold the work-

piece to it. Clamp the jig upside down (that is, with the clamps facing down) to your bench. Using a bottom-bearing bit on your plunge router, cut out the waste (see **photo G**).

3. Repeat this process for the other seven edging strips.

Cutting grooves for biscuits

Biscuits are used for vertical alignment of the edging, but a biscuit cutter can't cut slots on round edges. Instead you'll use a wing cutter to cut ⁵⁄₃₂-in. grooves in the table and edging strips.

1. Mount a wing cutter onto your router, and adjust the depth of the bottom of the bit to ³⁄₈ in. below the bottom of the router base (see the Edge Treatment Detail on p. 143). This positions the slot below the center so that when you cut the edge treatment you won't cut into the biscuit slots.

2. With the tabletop facing up, run the router counterclockwise all the way around the table.

3. Clamp the curved-pattern jig upside down to your bench again, and put an edge piece back into it. Position the cutter so the bottom of the blade is about ²⁵⁄₆₄ in. below the top sur-

Photo H: Use the jig to hold the workpiece for mitering. The stop at the right stabilizes the jig while still allowing me to microadjust its position. A paper shim microadjusts the angle.

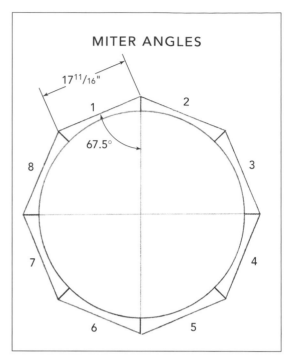

MITER ANGLES

$17^{11}/_{16}$"

67.5°

Cutting the miters

In theory, each of the eight edging strips is $17^{11}/_{16}$ in. long with a 67½-degree miter on each end. However, the diameter of the table will not be exact (in fact, the table probably won't be exactly round), the workpiece dimensions will never be perfect, and the adjustments used to cut the miters won't be perfect either. You'll have to microadjust the miters to account for these discrepancies.

Use the same jig you used to cut the negative edge and the biscuit slot to hold the edging for the miter cuts. Place paper shims between it and the miter gauge to microadjust the miter angle (see **photo H**). It's important to keep the workpieces symmetrical so the miters point straight into the center of the tabletop. Be sure to mark the order and orientation of the pieces as you go.

You'll first cut edging pieces 1, 3, 5, and 7 (the pieces are numbered in clockwise order) and glue them on in pairs, aligning the miters with the gluelines in the veneer so they appear to come directly out of the center of the table. Then you'll cut pieces 2 and 6 and glue them on. Finally, you'll cut 4 and 8 to complete the process. Step-by-step instructions follow, but

face of the edge piece. This will raise the level of the edging slightly above the level of the tabletop, allowing you to sand the edging without going through the veneer in the center. The exact position of your bit depends on the thickness of the stock you used to make the jig; you'll need to calculate this measurement for yourself.

4. Rout the grooves in the edging pieces. Be careful of the bit—it's large and fully exposed. Sweep up the dust as you go so you don't slip.

CLAMPING SEQUENCE FOR EDGING

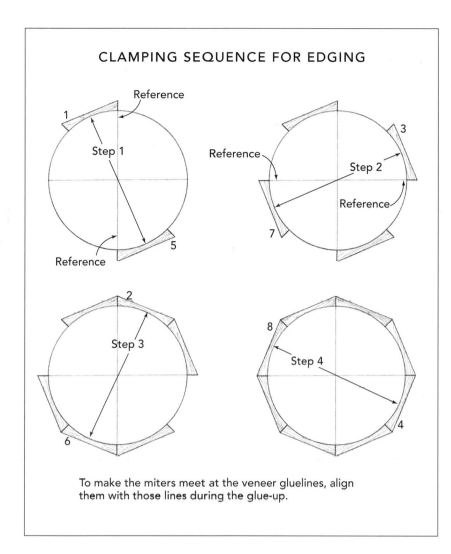

To make the miters meet at the veneer gluelines, align them with those lines during the glue-up.

PATTERN FOR THE EDGE MITER

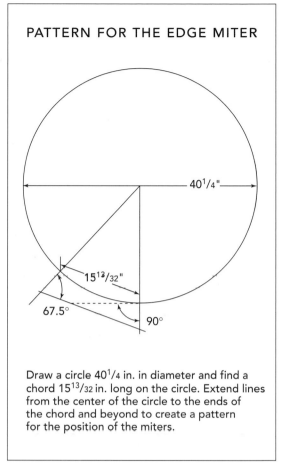

Draw a circle 40¹/₄ in. in diameter and find a chord 15¹³/₃₂ in. long on the circle. Extend lines from the center of the circle to the ends of the chord and beyond to create a pattern for the position of the miters.

you'll find that the work is fussy and not really amenable to doing "by the numbers." You'll have to adjust the variables as you go to get a good fit. It helps to have extra pieces of edging to make test cuts on.

1. Begin by either enlarging the illustration at right above to full size or redrawing it. Paste it to the cutting jig, aligning the curved edges, to show the position and angle of the miter and the length of the edging in relationship to the miter.

2. Set a stop and cut the first miter on the first workpiece, using paper shims to sneak up on the correct length and the miter angle.

3. Reverse the first workpiece and reset your stop to cut the second miter. Repeat for workpieces 3, 5, and 7.

4. Glue and clamp pieces 1 and 5 to the table, aligning the miters with the glueline in the veneer. Use two #20 biscuits for each edge piece. Spread glue on the edges and into the biscuit slot. When the glue is set, glue on pieces 3 and 7.

5. Cut the miters for workpiece 2 on the jig, leaving the piece a little long. As long as the workpiece is symmetrical, you'll be able to tell whether the miters are correct. If they're not, microadjust the miter angle until the angle is correct, then take off the waste from either end until the negative curve fits perfectly against the table.

6. Repeat the process with piece number 6. When they're complete, glue pieces 2 and 6 to the table.

7. Repeat steps 5 and 6 for pieces 4 and 8.

1. Spread a heavy layer of PVA onto one sheet of black veneer, then place a sheet of white over it. Spread glue on the white and put a sheet of mahogany over that. Follow with another sheet of white and another sheet of black. Clamp the sandwich together between two ¾-in. melamine cauls on your bench.
2. When the stack is dry, joint one edge using the veneer jointer jig and a flush trimming bit.
3. Put a Hi-AT veneer blade onto your table saw with a zero-clearance throat plate. Set the fence to ⅛ in., and raise the blade so the teeth are just barely above the level of the inlay.
4. Cut ⅛-in. strips of inlay using a sacrificial push stick (see **photo I**).

Installing the inlay

If you have any gaps between the edging and the veneer, the inlay will hide them.

1. Use your pivot jig and a ⅛-in. downward spiral bit to rout a ¹⁄₁₆-in.-deep groove at the joint between the veneer and the solid edge.
2. Remove the center pivot piece carefully so as not to damage the veneer. Don't pry up the center square; try twisting it off. If that doesn't work, use lacquer thinner to loosen the tape.
3. Cut one end of the inlay square with a sharp chisel, making sure the bevel faces away from the inlay (see **photo J**).
4. Lay the inlay into the groove, starting at one miter, and cut it to length at the next miter joint. The inlay should bend easily around the curved groove. You will need to scrape the edges with a cabinet scraper to get it to fit properly; be sure to scrape both edges evenly (see **photo K**).
5. Glue in the first piece with PVA, and wipe out the excess glue in the groove.
6. Continue around the table, fitting and gluing the inlay piece by piece until it's complete (see **photo L**). Each new piece of inlay should butt cleanly with the last, and the bands of color should not have any offset between one piece and the next. If you think matching the colors will be too difficult, lay up a solid-color inlay and use that instead.

Cutting the edging round

1. Using the router on the pivot that you used to cut the veneered part of the table to round, cut the edging round in several shallow passes. When you're about ¼ in. into the table, cut off the waste with a bandsaw or jigsaw. Don't remove the pivot point yet.
2. Using a top-bearing flush trimming bit, turn the table over and trim it round.

Making the inlay

You'll make an inlay from five leaves of colored veneer (black, white, mahogany, white, black) sandwiched together to make a pattern. Since veneer has a standard thickness, when it's glued together the sandwich remains uniformly thick.

Photo K: The inlay probably won't fit the slot at first. Scrape both sides evenly with a scraper, testing the fit as you go.

Photo L: Once you get the inlay into the slot and aligned with one miter, cut it to length by eyeballing the second miter and scribing it with a chisel. Don't remove the inlay completely; place a piece of scrap ¼-in. ply under it and cut it to length using the line you scribed.

Making the subtop

Edge-band the subtop using a hot iron and a hardwood block, then sand with 150-grit paper.

Milling the edge treatment

Hog out the waste, cutting left to right. Take one last, very shallow pass, climb cutting around the edge of the table to get a fine cut.

FINISHING UP

Assembly

1. Glue the floating tenons into the cross braces, then glue the cross braces to the legs, making sure the lap joints in the cross braces are oriented so they will fit together. Measure across the diagonals to verify that the structures are square.

2. Once the two leg assemblies are dry, put the lap joint together. Sand the cross braces, then glue the lap joint together.

3. Predrill the subtop and cross braces for screws, using #8 by 2-in. steel wood screws, and screw the cross braces to the subtop.

4. Predrill and screw the subtop to the tabletop, using #8 by 1¼-in. steel wood screws.

Sanding

Using a random-orbit sander, sand the center of the tabletop to 150 grit, then sand the edging by hand. Check to make sure you haven't missed anything.

Finishing

High-end tables like this one should be sprayed with lacquer if possible. If you do not have spray equipment, finish it with a hand-applied gel varnish. See appendix 1 on pp. 178–179 for more information on finishing.

BOAT-SHAPED PEDESTAL TABLE

The boat shape became popular for conference tables when researchers found that people seated at curved tables could see and hear each other better than people at long, straight tables. More recently, dining-table designers have also begun to use the boat shape, on the theory that it's just as important to talk to your family and friends at dinner as it is to talk to your colleagues at meetings.

I've designed this modern boat-shaped dining table to demonstrate torsion-box technology and other modern construction techniques. Torsion boxes, which are constructed on the same principles as airplane wings, are easy and inexpensive to build with honeycomb paper products and a vacuum press. Because torsion-box tabletops have a high strength-to-weight ratio, are very flat, and can support heavy loads cantilevered off an edge, they offer design possibilities unavailable with sheet goods or solid wood.

While this table is designed for a modern, formal setting, you can easily change the design to fit your own needs and tastes. I've used satinwood, but many other species of veneer would be appropriate. Using a dark veneer on the pedestal with a lighter veneer on top would make the top appear to float.

Boat-Shaped Pedestal Table

THE PEDESTALS FOR THE BOAT-SHAPED PEDESTAL TABLE are made with veneered panels cut at compound-mitered angles. Aprons fit into slots in the pedestals and are biscuit-joined to apron ends that are secured to the insides of the pedestals. The pedestal top, which fits over the pedestal assembly, is screwed into the table subtop and the tabletop. The built-up edging on the torsion-box tabletop hides the subtop and the pedestal top.

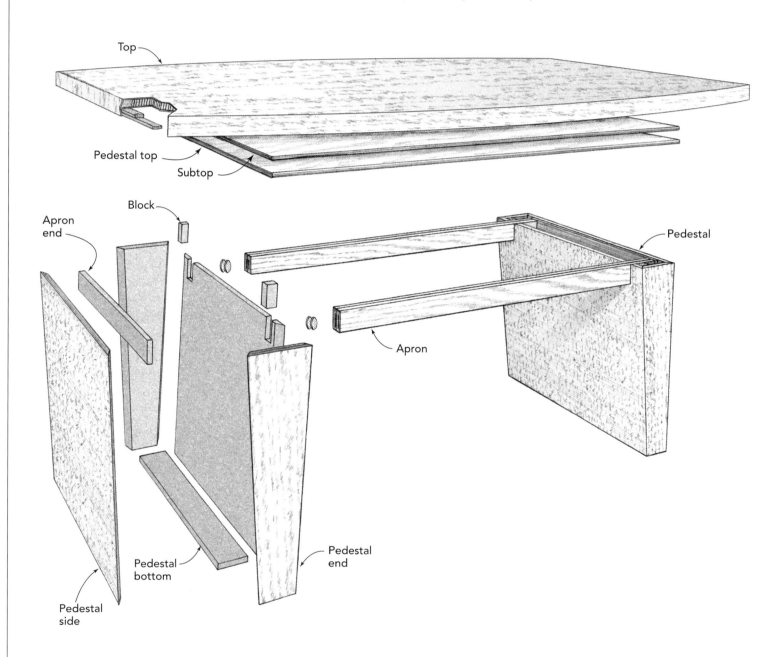

Top

Pedestal top

Subtop

Block

Apron
end

Pedestal

Apron

Pedestal
bottom

Pedestal
end

Pedestal
side

TOP VIEW

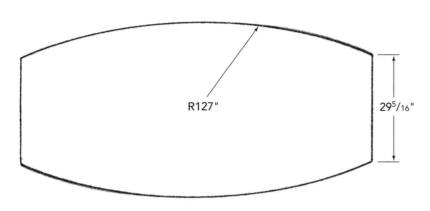

R127"

29⁵/₁₆"

PEDESTAL DETAIL (FRONT VIEW)

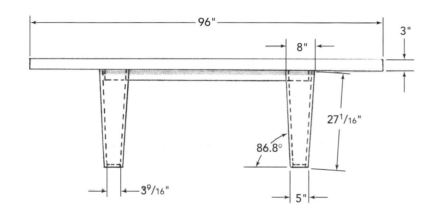

96"

3"

8"

27¹/₁₆"

86.8°

3⁹/₁₆"

5"

PEDESTAL DETAIL (SIDE VIEW)

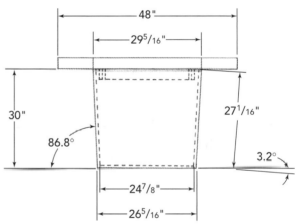

48"

29⁵/₁₆"

30"

27¹/₁₆"

86.8°

3.2°

24⁷/₈"

26⁵/₁₆"

ANATOMY OF THE TABLETOP

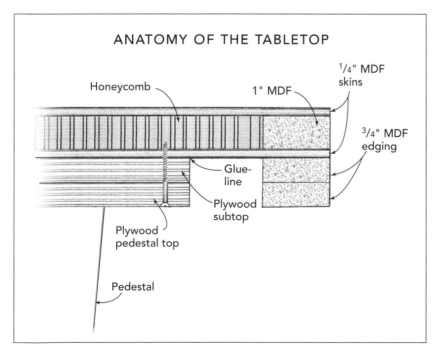

Honeycomb

1" MDF

¹/₄" MDF skins

³/₄" MDF edging

Glue-line

Plywood subtop

Plywood pedestal top

Pedestal

Building the Table Step-by-Step

Cut List for Boat-Shaped Pedestal Table

Table Parts		
2	Faces for tabletop	96 in. x 48 in. (¼-in. MDF)
1	Resin-impregnated cardboard honeycomb[1]	96 in. x 48 in. x 1 in.
8	Side edging strips	52³⁄₁₆ in. x 5 in. (¾-in. MDF)
4	End edging strips	29½ in. x 2 in. (¾-in. MDF)
4	Torsion-box side edgings	52³⁄₁₆ in. x 5 in. (1-in. MDF)
2	Torsion-box end edgings	29½ in. x 2 in. (1-in. MDF)
2	Pedestal tops and subtops	61⅝ in. x 32⁵⁄₁₆ in. (¾-in. birch plywood)
4	Pedestal sides	29⁵⁄₁₆ in. x 27¹⁄₁₆ in. (¾-in. MDF)
4	Pedestal ends	27¹⁄₁₆ in. x 8 in. (¾-in. MDF)
2	Pedestal bottoms	24⅞ in. x 3⁹⁄₁₆ in. (¾-in. MDF)
2	Aprons	57⅛ in. x 3 in. x 1½ in. (¾-in. birch plywood)
2	Apron ends	25½ in. x 3 in. (¾-in. birch plywood)
4	Blocks	1¼ in. x 3 in. x 1½ in. (¾-in. birch)
Veneer		
1	Tabletop (top and ends)	108 in. x 48 in. (satinwood)
1	Tabletop (bottom)	96 in. x 48 in. (mahogany backer veneer/paper-backed veneer)[2]
2	Tabletop (sides)	108 in. x 5 in.
4	Pedestal sides (outer)	29⁵⁄₁₆ in. x 27¹⁄₁₆ in. (satinwood)
4	Pedestal ends (outer)	27¹⁄₁₆ in. x 8 in. (satinwood)
4	Pedestal sides (inner)	29⁵⁄₁₆ in. x 27¹⁄₁₆ in. (mahogany backer veneer/paper-backed veneer)
4	Pedestal ends (inner)	27¹⁄₁₆ in. x 8 in. (mahogany backer veneer/paper-backed veneer)
2	Aprons (outer)	57⅛ in. x 3 in. (satinwood)
2	Aprons (inner)	57⅛ in. x 3 in. (mahogany backer veneer/paper-backed veneer)
Material for Construction Process		
1	Top caul	96 in. x 48 in. (¼-in. melamine)
Other Materials		
20	Steel wood screws	#10 x 2 in.
4	Levelers with tee-nuts	⁵⁄₁₆ in.
100	Biscuits	#20

[1]See Sources of Supply on p. 183.

[2]You may be able to buy single 4-ft. by 8-ft. sheets of veneer, already laid up, with a paper backing. If you can find one, you won't have to lay up the backer veneer.

You'll start by making the tabletop assembly: constructing the torsion box, veneering it, and cutting the final boat profile. You'll then attach and veneer the edge and add the subtop, which helps attach the torsion box to the pedestals. Next, construct and attach the pedestals to the aprons and pedestal top. Finally, attach the tabletop to the base.

BUILDING THE TABLETOP

To build the torsion box, you'll lay up the 2-in.- and 5-in.-wide edging strips to form the table outline and then use the outline of the edging as a guide to rough-cut the tabletop panels. Then you'll assemble the torsion box, pressing it in the vacuum press. You'll lay up the veneer and put the assembly back into the vacuum press to glue it, and then cut it to final shape. Finally, you'll attach and veneer the built-up edge. Although traditional veneering generally calls for edges to be veneered before the tops, the advent of modern glues and vacuum presses allows a top-first approach.

Cutting the edging

Follow the cutting diagram shown at right to cut the edging strips. This will leave scrap pieces suitable for the jigs and cauls you will need.

Rough-cutting the tabletop

1. Stack the ¼-in. sheet of melamine and the two ¼-in. sheets of MDF on your bench. Align the edges, then screw them together at the four corners with drywall screws. This allows you to cut out the two tabletop skins and the caul all at once.
2. Cut the miters in all three sets of edging strips. First make all the 52-degree cuts in the 2-in. pieces, then make all the 49-degree cuts. Finally, adjust the 79-degree cuts to get a good fit. Don't sweat the miters; if they're a little off, you'll fill in the gaps. The veneer covers everything.

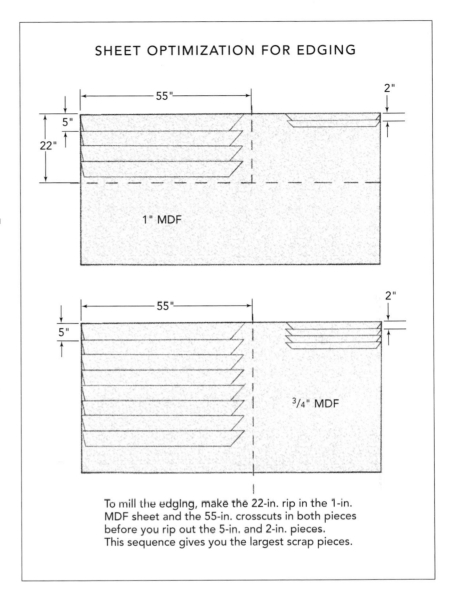

SHEET OPTIMIZATION FOR EDGING

1" MDF

¾" MDF

To mill the edging, make the 22-in. rip in the 1-in. MDF sheet and the 55-in. crosscuts in both pieces before you rip out the 5-in. and 2-in. pieces. This sequence gives you the largest scrap pieces.

3. Lay out one set of edging strips on your tabletop stack, as shown in the illustration on p. 164. Trace around the inside and outside of the edging with a pencil. Using a circular saw, cut the tabletop and caul to rough shape just outside the outer lines, then trim off the sharp-ended points where the side edging overhangs the ends.

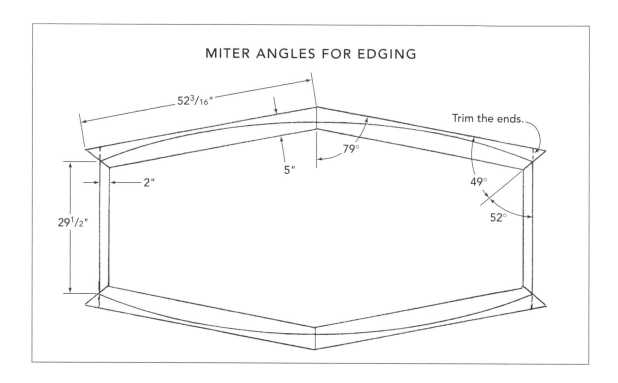

MITER ANGLES FOR EDGING

52³/₁₆"

Trim the ends.

79°

5"

2"

49°

29¹/₂"

52°

Photo A: Be sure to use resin-impregnated honeycomb made for torsion-box construction. Ordinary cardboard will collapse under vacuum pressure.

Dry-assembling the torsion box

1. Start by unscrewing the MDF and melamine sheets. Keep the sheet of MDF with the edging outlines on your bench and assemble the 1-in. edging onto it, using the lines you traced. Hold the edging in place using one or two drywall screws per piece, as needed. Reserve the two sets of ¾-in. edging strips for later.

2. On a table saw, cut the honeycomb to shape and lay it into the space created by the edging. The honeycomb should fit snugly—don't scrunch it, but don't leave gaps either (see **photo A**).

3. Put on the top skin and then the melamine caul (melamine side down), making sure their edges are even within about ⅛ in. Trim if necessary.

4. Round over the top edges and corners of the melamine sheet using a mill file and disassemble the stack.

Gluing up the torsion box

1. Set up the vacuum press, adjusting the vacuum pump to provide 10 Hg to 15 Hg of pressure instead of the usual 25 Hg, and

TORSION-BOX TECHNOLOGY

A torsion box is made of two thin skins with an internal structure between them. Traditionally, the internal structure was a lattice of wooden strips stapled together. Making a lattice isn't difficult, but it's a lot of work. Resin-impregnated cardboard honeycomb makes construction less expensive and faster. The structure's strength is in the gluelines between the honeycomb and the skins—the edging isn't needed for strength. Although the honeycomb is made of paper, the ends have enough glue surface to make a strong bond.

Because the honeycomb is hollow, even large torsion boxes aren't very heavy. However, they are extremely strong and rigid and won't sag when you place loads near the edge. This is useful for designs where there is no apron to keep the top rigid, or where there is a long overhang off the apron or legs.

Honeycomb is strong. Even though the walls are just thin paper, when it's made up into a honeycomb pattern the aggregate easily supports my weight without being damaged.

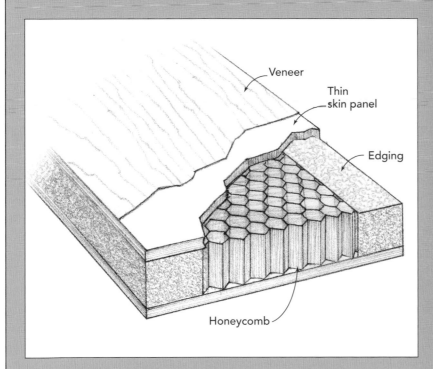

Veneer

Thin skin panel

Edging

Honeycomb

---

arrange the torsion-box components. It's important to make sure the platen is flat. Any irregularities will be telegraphed to the torsion box.
2. Mix up the glue (see p. 135 for more information on urea resin glue) and spread a heavy layer of it on the entire surface of the bottom skin.
3. Position the 1-in. edging, holding it in place with one or two 1-in. drywall screws screwed upward through the skin into each

Photo B: Available from any hardware store, automotive body filler can be used to fill cracks, dents, and screw holes in woodwork that will be painted or covered over.

piece of edging. Make sure the heads of the screws are below the surface of the skin so the skin sits flat on the platen.

4. Next, put the honeycomb into the space you left for it. Spread another thick layer of glue onto the bottom of the top skin and place it over the assembly.

5. Place the top caul on the torsion box, screwing it in place with two or three drywall screws—this will make it much easier to move the whole assembly into the vacuum bag. Make sure the screw heads are just below the surface of the caul so you won't damage the bag. Seal the bag and turn on the pump. Put excess glue into a piece of plastic wrap, and press the panel until the glue in the plastic wrap is hard.

6. After pressing, open the bag, take off the cauls, and stand the torsion box up overnight so air can circulate around it. If you leave it in the bag, the moisture escaping from the glue might cause the box to warp. Remove any remaining screws the next morning.

Veneering the torsion box

Jointing, laying up, and pressing veneer are described on pp. 128–136. The top of this table should be book-matched; the match under the table is unimportant.

1. Cut the satinwood veneer for the top 12 in. long, then joint and lay it up in a book-match.

2. Once the top veneer is laid up, carefully crosscut 4 in. off each end with a mat knife and straightedge. These pieces will be used for the ends of the table. Label them so you know which piece goes on which end and in which direction.

3. If you don't have paper-backed backer veneer, joint and lay up the backer veneer for the table bottom. To cut the veneer to rough size, place a caul over each laid-up sheet, and run a line of veneer tape just outside the outline of the caul. (If you have paper-backed veneer for the bottom, you won't need the tape.) Cut the veneer through the tape with a mat knife. The veneer tape will keep the edges from fraying and make moving the sheet of veneer easy.

4. Remove any screws in the torsion box and fill the holes with automotive body filler (see **photo B**). Sand the surface flush.

5. Using urea resin glue, press the bottom veneer and then the top veneer. The veneer will break cleanly over the edge when it's pressed. (If you want, you can press both the top and bottom veneer at the same time. Use a bottom caul to make transfer into the bag easy.)

Cutting the boat shape

The tabletop's curve is an arc of a 127-in. circle. To cut the arc, make a pattern from the leftover 1-in. MDF, using a router on a compass as described on pp. 94–95, then use the pattern to pattern-rout the tabletop. See p. 49 for details on patternmaking.

1. Using scrap, make a 127-in. compass.
2. Attach the cutoff piece from the 1-in. MDF to the floor. I have a wooden floor and can simply screw the panel down. If you can't do that, hold the panel in place by some other means, such as hot glue or double-faced tape.
3. Secure the pivot to the floor. Turn on the router and, with several passes, cut into the panel until you're almost all the way through. Be careful not to cut into the floor.
4. Place the pattern on your workbench and cut off the waste using a jigsaw, then use a flush trimming bit to rout off the last bit of waste.
5. Place the tabletop on your bench, position the pattern on it, and clamp it in place.
6. Mount a ½-in. downward-spiral bit in your router with a guide bushing in the baseplate. Run the bushing against the pattern, cutting down about ⅟₁₆ in., or just through the veneer. The bushing will leave the cut edge slightly proud of the pattern.
7. Cut off the waste using a jigsaw with a long blade.
8. Using a bottom-bearing flush trimming bit, run it first against the pattern and then against the table to rout the remainder of the edge flush.

Adding the edging and subtop

1. Place a blanket on your bench, and turn the tabletop upside down on it. Position the edging around the table, clamp it, and use drywall screws to hold it in place.
2. Removing the screws from one section at a time, spread PVA on the glue surfaces. Screw the sections back in place, and clamp them to the tabletop with cauls on both sides. The cauls will distribute even clamp pressure on the workpieces and keep you from marring the surface of the table. Continue around the table until all of the edging is glued in place.
3. When the glue is dry, remove the screws. Cut off the waste using a jigsaw.

IRONING ON VENEER

Since PVA is water based, it cures by evaporation; the hotter it is, the faster it dries. Veneer is thin enough so that if you heat its surface with a normal household iron, the heat is transferred through the veneer to the glue. The glue grabs almost immediately and the flat iron acts as a press. The iron should be hot enough to heat the glue but not hot enough to scorch the veneer—you can experiment to find the correct heat setting. This technique works well on narrow, convex surfaces that are hard to clamp without elaborate cauls, although good cauls do work better.

Put a heavy glueline on the substrate (use enough glue to get squeeze-out, which will bubble as it heats), then place the veneer over it. Begin at one end, holding the hot iron in place. As the glue begins to grab, move the iron slowly and evenly along the veneer. To squeeze out as much excess glue as possible, rub a piece of hardwood with a rounded-over edge against the veneer while the glue is still hot and liquid.

Don't borrow the household iron. Buy an inexpensive one just for the shop.

Photo C: Ironing on veneer is too much work on large, flat panels—a vacuum press works much better. For curved edgebanding, however, it's easier than making negative cauls, the only other option.

4. Use a flush trimming bit with the bearing running against the tabletop to rout the edging.

5. Fill any gaps at the miters with automotive body filler and sand them flush.

6. Center the subtop inside the edging, trimming it as needed.

7. Spread glue on the underside of the tabletop and the subtop, then screw the subtop to the bottom of the table. The screws will act as clamps until the glue dries.

Veneering the edge

Because the edging is so thick, you can ignore the "balanced panel" rule for once and veneer only the outside. The veneer on the long sides of the table runs horizontally, and you'll attach it using an iron-on technique with yellow glue (see the sidebar on p. 167). On the ends, where the grain runs vertically, you'll use PVA again and clamp the veneer in place with cauls.

1. Rough-cut all the veneer to length and width.

2. To veneer the sides, set your iron to "cotton." Make sure the iron has no water in it and turn off the steam.

3. Place the tabletop right side up on your bench, and paint the first foot of the side edging with a thick layer of PVA.

4. Put the veneer in place and hold the iron directly on it, pressing it down onto the edge. As you work, adjust the heat up or down as needed. Continue along the edge, painting on glue as necessary. Repeat with the other edge (see **photo C**). When the glue is completely dry, use a mill file to slice off the excess veneer, as shown in **photo D**.

5. To veneer the ends, use the laid-up bookmatched veneer reserved from the tabletop. Spread PVA on both ends, and carefully position the veneer to match the top. Put a heavy caul on each end, and clamp across the tabletop and bottom to get even pressure on the caul (see **photo E**). When the glue is dry, trim the edges using a mill file.

Photo D: Hold the mill file at a slight angle, and use its teeth to slice off excess veneer.

Photo E: Clamping over and under the table gives even pressure on the cauls.

BUILDING THE PEDESTALS

Making the parts

To make the pedestal parts, you will cut the substrate into parts, stack them in the press to veneer them, then cut the miters. The veneer on the side panels is book-matched. To obtain a clean cut on the veneered panels, you'll need a table-saw blade designed for veneered panels (see Sources of Supply on p. 183).

1. Cut out rectangular panels for the pedestal parts, following the illustration on p. 170.
2. Lay up the veneer for the fronts and backs of the panels, book-matching the satinwood veneer for the pedestal sides.
3. Cut top and bottom cauls out of ¼-in. melamine the same size as the sides and end panels.
4. Mix urea resin and lay up the stack of end panels in the following order, bottom to top: bottom caul, mahogany backer, end panel, satinwood, waxed paper, mahogany backer, end panel, satinwood, waxed paper, . . . , top caul.

5. Place the stack into the vacuum bag, and turn on the pump to hold it in place while you lay up the sides in the same manner.
6. Open the bag and press both stacks, leaving plenty of room around the sides of each stack. Let them sit overnight before you process them any further.
7. Since the tops and bottoms of the sides and ends have a 3.2-degree bevel, set your sawblade to that angle and your fence to ½ in. over final dimension, then run your side panels through to cut off the top edges of the sides. Make sure all the grain on the side panels is oriented in the same direction.
8. Set a stop on a miter gauge, and cut the top edges of the end panels.
9. Reset your fence to final dimensions, then turn your panels over and cut the bottom edges of the sides. Make sure the top and bottom angles run parallel.
10. Reset the stop on your miter gauge, and cut the bottom edges of the end panels.

Sheet Optimization for Pedestals

WITH THE TABLE-SAW FENCE set at 30¼ in., rip pieces for three of the pedestal sides. The fourth side can be made from the cutoff from the ¾-in. edging. Reset the fence to 28¾ in. and crosscut the sides. Finally, set the fence to 8⅞ in. and rip the ends.

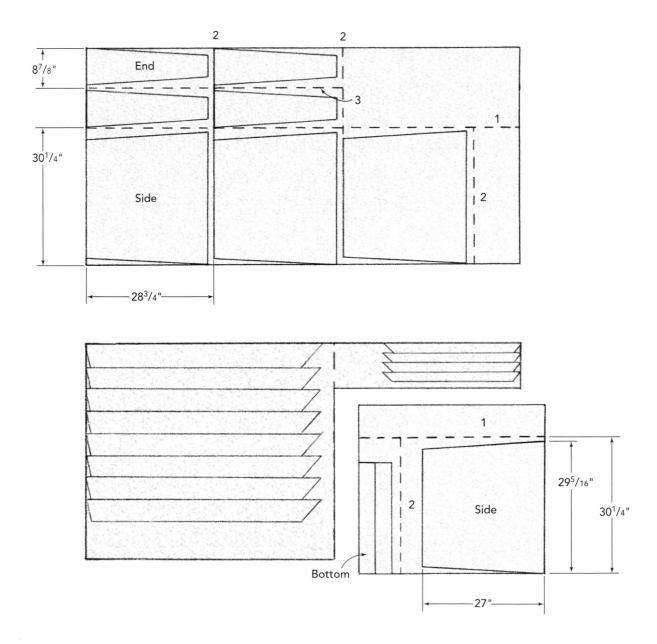

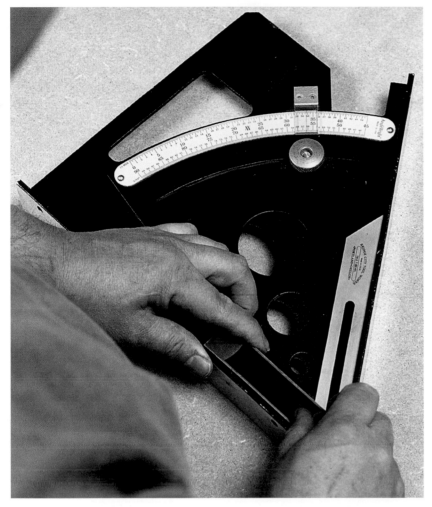

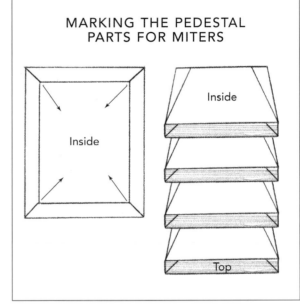

Photo F: This large protractor has a tolerance of ¹⁄₂₀ degree and is useful for machine setup of nonstandard angles.

MARKING THE PEDESTAL PARTS FOR MITERS

Inside

Inside

Top

Cutting the compound miters

Cutting compound miters is hard. Not only do you have to figure out what angles to cut, but you also have to cut everything in the right direction. Keeping everything straight is the most difficult part. Be organized and systematic, and, most important, mark the angles and direction of all cuts, using pencil or lumber crayon so the marks won't rub off. Exaggerate the angles so you won't make any mistakes. Before cutting anything, make sure the workpiece is oriented correctly.

These directions assume that you're running the miter gauge on the left of the blade using a right-tilt table saw. If you have a left-tilt table saw, cut to the right of the saw and

reverse the clock directions. This way you can keep the panel right side up, giving a cleaner cut.

1. Stack up the sides and ends so the good edges are oriented the same way. Orient any tearout on the crosscut edges toward the top so it will be hidden under the table.
2. Mark the miter angle on the tops of the panels. Remember that miters are always angled toward the inside.
3. Mark the taper on the insides of the panels. This taper runs from top to bottom.
4. Setting your protractor to 44.9 degrees, transfer that angle to a bevel gauge (see **photo F**). Set the angle of your table-saw blade to the bevel gauge, as shown in **photo G**.

Tip: Since tiny measurement errors can cause visible gaps in mitered joints, it's important to use a protractor with a tolerance of ¹⁄₁₀ degree or better.

Photo G: Raise the blade to full height and angle it until the light between the blade and bevel gauge disappears.

Tip: Don't cut the miters on the pedestal ends without using the sled.

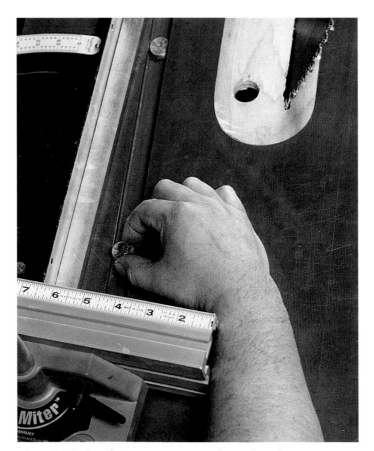

Photo H: Raise the miter gauge with stacks of pennies so your protractor will have a reference edge on both the fence and the bar and can accurately transfer the angle.

Next, set the protractor to 3.2 degrees. Using Mark Duginske's trick, raise the miter gauge up in its slot by stacking a couple of pennies into the miter-gauge slot. Place the miter gauge on the pennies to raise it slightly above the level of the table, as shown in **photo H**. (And you thought pennies weren't useful!) Set the miter gauge to the protractor, turning the miter gauge counterclockwise. Remove the pennies.

5. Since the panels are too large to sit in front of the blade with the miter gauge behind them, turn the miter gauge 180 degrees and put it in the slot backward and to the left of the blade so you can push against it.

6. Butt the top of one pedestal side against the fence, outside up. Set a stop to cut the panel so that the center seam of the veneer is centered. After verifying the orientation of the board, make the cut. Repeat the process for the other three sides. The pedestal ends are too long and thin to register safely against the miter gauge, so they must be carried on a sled. Clamp one end piece to the miter-gauge sled jig shown on p. 177 with toggle clamps, then set a stop and clamp the sled to the fence. Make the cut. Repeat the process for the other three ends.

Photo I: To position the slot far enough into the miter so that the cut won't go through the side of the panel, you might need to add a shim to the fence.

7. Raise the miter gauge back up on the pennies, and, with the protractor set to 3.2 degrees, reset the miter gauge, this time turning it clockwise. Remove the pennies.

8. Set a stop on your miter gauge, and place the bottom of one of the pedestal sides against the fence, outside up. Make the second cut on the side pieces, adjusting your stop to the correct width. Repeat the process for the remaining three sides.

9. Readjust the fence on the sled and set a stop on it. Clamp the sled against the fence, and run it through the blade without anything on it, adjusting your stop until you get the correct width.

10. Butt the bottom of a pedestal end against the fence on the sled, outside up. Clamp it in place and make your cut. Repeat for the remaining three ends.

Cutting the biscuit joints

1. Mark the pedestal ends and sides for six biscuit slots in each mitered surface (see pp. 111–114 for instructions on biscuit joinery).

2. Carefully position the biscuit-cutter fence and cut the slots. You might need to add a shim to the fence to position the slot far enough away from the edge (see **photo I**).

Gluing up the pedestal

Because it's hard to get good clamp pressure clamping across compound-mitered joints, use cauls to glue up the pedestals (see the illustration on p. 174).

1. Do a dry glue-up first, putting biscuits in the slots, clamping the cauls to the panels, and dry-clamping the whole assembly.

Tip: For this or any other glue-up that's going to take a long time to complete, I use white PVA, which has a slightly longer open time than yellow PVA.

Tip: In order not to mar the veneer when you're nailing brads, disconnect the air line from your nail gun, then wrap the safety tip with a triple thickness of masking tape.

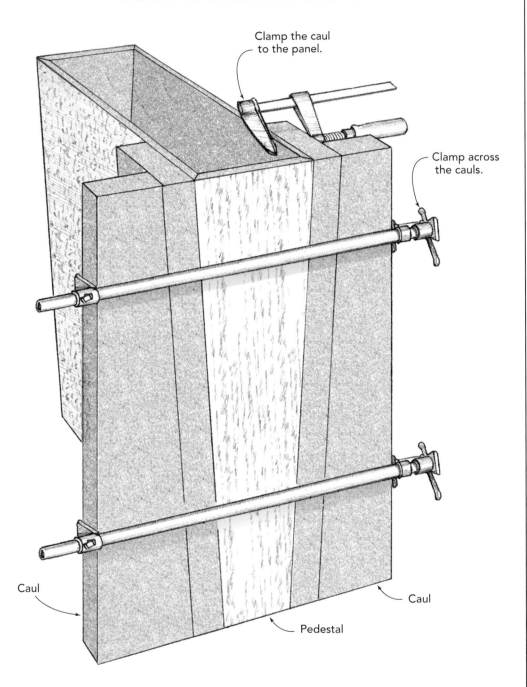

Clamp the caul to the panel.

Clamp across the cauls.

Caul

Caul

Pedestal

Clamping compound-mitered assemblies is difficult because the cauls slip. Clamp the cauls to the pedestal so they can't move and use deep throat clamps, or cut notches if you need to in the cauls so your clamps will clear the caul edges. Don't skimp on the clamps or you'll leave gaps in the miters. Work out your sequence during a dry glue-up. Note that each edge needs two mirror-image cauls, making a total of eight cauls per pedestal.

2. Once you're satisfied with the sequence, spread glue on the mitered surfaces and in the slots.

3. Place biscuits in the slots and glue the assembly together.

Cutting the pedestal bottom

Dimensions for the pedestal bottoms are approximate and will vary with the thickness of the backer veneer. You should take actual measurements from the glued-up pedestal.

1. Setting the sawblade to 3.2 degrees, trim the base to size (where the edges are tilted, as in this piece, you cut the larger surface to the given dimensions). Use a short piece of scrap to measure the width, then cut the workpiece. Sneak up on the length using a stop and paper shims.

2. Predrill for and install two tee-nuts in each pedestal bottom to hold levelers. You can install the levelers when the table is done.

3. Put glue on both surfaces and glue the bottoms in. Shoot 18-gauge, 1½-in. brads to hold them in place, orienting the brad heads vertically.

COMPLETING THE PEDESTAL ASSEMBLY

Making the aprons

This table has only long aprons, since the pedestals replace the short aprons. To build the aprons, face-glue the two pieces of ¾-in. birch ply together and press them in the vacuum press. If you round over the edges of the top board, you won't need a caul.

1. Lay up and press face and backer veneer onto the apron panel with the grain running horizontally.

2. Rip the aprons out of the panel to width, leaving them long, and sand them.

Cutting slots in the pedestals

This step was postponed until the aprons were sanded to final thickness, so you can make the slots to fit them exactly. As a safety precaution, always keep more than half of the workpiece against the fence of the miter gauge. To do this, move the miter gauge between left- and right-hand slots.

1. Raise the table-saw blade to the width of the apron.

2. Running the miter gauge to the left of the blade, set a stop and cut one side of the far slot in one pedestal. Make the same cut in the other pedestal.

3. Reset the stop and cut the other side of the far slot in one pedestal. Waste away the middle by making repeated passes between the two side cuts. Repeat the process for the other pedestal.

4. Transfer the miter gauge to the right side of the blade, and repeat the process to cut the other slot.

Making and attaching the apron ends and interior screw blocks

To attach the aprons to the pedestals, you'll biscuit the aprons to apron ends, which you'll then glue to the insides of the pedestals. Additional interior screw blocks strengthen the connection between aprons and pedestals.

1. Dimension the apron ends and the interior screw blocks. You should be able to cut the blocks from the apron cutoffs.

2. Glue the blocks to the pedestals.

3. Sand the pedestals.

4. Biscuit-join the apron ends to the aprons, using a double row of biscuit slots.

5. Spread glue on the ends of the blocks, then glue and screw the apron ends to the insides of the pedestals.

6. Screw through the aprons into the blocks.

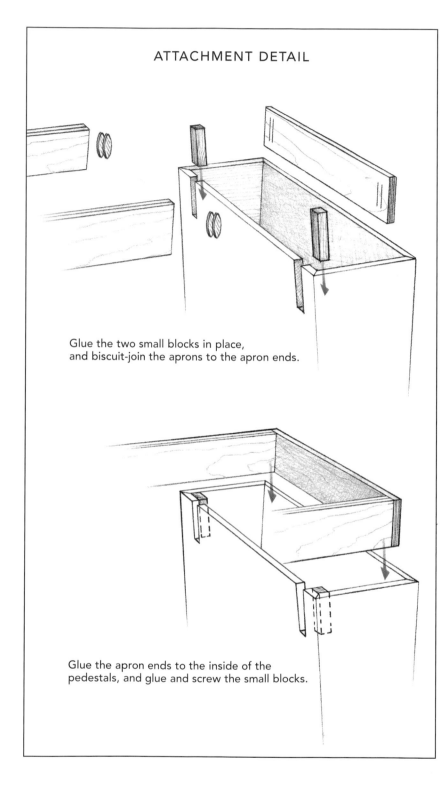

ATTACHMENT DETAIL

Glue the two small blocks in place,
and biscuit-join the aprons to the apron ends.

Glue the apron ends to the inside of the
pedestals, and glue and screw the small blocks.

Making and attaching the pedestal top

1. Cut out the subtop and pedestal top, which are two identical panels. Place one of the two panels on your bench, and turn the pedestal assembly upside down on top of it. Center the pedestal assembly on the plywood, and outline the pedestals and aprons with a pencil. Place the pedestal on the floor, aligning the top over it.

2. Snap chalk lines onto the plywood to show the position of the aprons underneath. Predrill for 3-in. wood screws every 6 in. along the lines.

3. Remove the top, turn it upside down, and sand up to the lines. Round the corners over using a roundover bit. Spread yellow glue inside the outline of the pedestal and on the upper edges of the pedestal and apron.

4. Put the top on the pedestal again and screw it down.

FINISHING UP

Attaching the top

1. Place the top on the pedestal, aligning the subtop with the pedestal top.

2. Predrill for #10 by 2-in. steel wood screws, and screw the pedestal to the tabletop. You can disassemble the table for transport by removing the screws.

Sanding

1. Sand the top and pedestal using a random-orbit sander to 150 grit, being careful not to go through the veneer or damage the edges.

2. Holding a cabinet scraper burnisher at a 45-degree angle, press hard against the edges where the veneer meets to soften them.

3. Go over every inch of the table with a hand-sanding block, looking for defects.

Finishing

Fill the brad holes in the pedestal with colored wax. See appendix 1 on pp. 178–179 for details on finishing.

MITER-GAUGE SLED

This sled, made from a scrap piece of ¾-in. sheet stock, should be as wide as the fence on your miter gauge. The reference fence needs to be more than ¾ in. thick so the miter will reference against it without riding up the edge. Screw the reference fence to it, perpendicular to the miter-gauge fence and a little more than 8 in. off the edge. (Don't glue the reference fence in place.) Add two fast-acting toggle clamps to the reference fence, and clamp the sled to the miter-gauge fence, as shown in the photo at right.

After cutting the first miter, unscrew the fence and reattach it as shown in the photo below, using the same protractor setup you used to adjust the miter gauge. Clamp the sled back to the miter gauge.

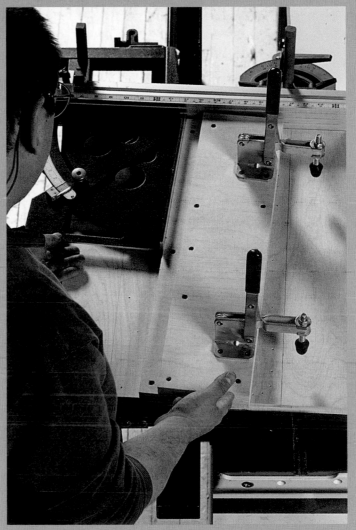

Add a second layer to the reference fence so the miter registers against it (or build it that way in the first place). Adjust the fence angle using the angle already set on the protractor, turn the miter gauge, and recut the miter. Don't try cutting this miter without the sled.

Fast-acting toggle clamps are very useful in making jigs. Their rubber ends won't mar the workpiece, and they keep your hands away from the sawblade.

APPENDIX 1: FINISHING

There are two main reasons for finishing furniture. One is to protect it. Dining tables, more than most pieces of furniture, need to be protected from spilled food and drink, and hot and dropped plates. A good finish should protect the surface from heat, water, and alcohol and protect the underlying structure of the table. Veneer especially needs protection.

The other major reason for finishing is to enhance the beauty of the table. Without finishing, wood appears dull and lifeless. Finish brightens and highlights the beauty of the wood. In highly figured wood, finishing brings out the movement in the figure.

I would like to make a personal plea against using stain. Many people confuse staining with finishing and believe that you must stain in order to finish. That's not true. Staining, which colors the wood, is sometimes needed to match a replacement part to a restored antique. On new pieces, however, it is unnecessary. Most stains, other than chemical stains, are just thin paint; the pigment particles obscure the wood's luminosity and mask the natural patina process. Unless stain is used in the hands of an expert, the result often looks cheap. In addition, staining is difficult; it's hard to get good and consistent results. So unless you have a specific reason to stain, skip the step and move directly on to applying a finish.

Finishing requires more care than any other step. In general, woodworking is forgiving. Most mistakes are easily fixable; at worst, you may have to replace a part. But since the finish is the surface of the product, any flaw is immediately apparent.

Finishing Options

There are five major classes of finish: shellac, varnish, oil, lacquer, and advanced modern finishes such as polyester and catalyzed varnish. The classes differ in their levels of protection and in their appearance. Shellac, while beautiful, is not appropriate for dining tables because it doesn't offer enough protection. The advanced finishes are good looking and offer the most protection. However, they are very toxic, they can only be applied with spray equipment in a fireproof spray booth, and they require specialized knowledge and practice to apply. If you want to use one of the modern finishes, consider sending your table out to be sprayed.

If you want to do your own finishing, you have three main options: oil, varnish, or lacquer. Each of these has myriad formulations and brand names. In general, oil and varnish can be applied by hand (with a rag or brush), while lacquer should be sprayed for best effect. If you don't have spray equipment, use some formulation of oil or varnish. Since varnish offers far more protection than a pure oil finish, that's the finish I recommend for dining tables.

The majority of the designers of the tables in this book used either Sutherland Welles' polymerized tung oil or Bartley's gel varnish (see Sources of Supply on p. 183). Polymerized tung oil is really a mixture of oil and varnish. Gel varnish is varnish in a gel emulsion, which is very easy to apply and builds quickly. Both of these products, and others like them, can be used successfully to finish any of the projects in this book. Simply follow the directions.

Sanding

The object of sanding is to remove mill marks and ready the surface for finish. If you do it correctly, the process isn't boring or difficult. It's fun and interesting to watch the grain reveal itself as you sand to progressively finer grits. Here are some sanding guidelines:

• Sanding the parts before assembling the table is easier than trying to get into the corners afterwards. (You'll still need to sand off the squeeze-out after gluing.)

- Start with a low grit—80 or 100—to remove mill marks rapidly, then move up to finer sandpaper.
- Don't oversand. If you start with 80-grit paper to remove the mill marks, sand just until the mill marks are gone, then stop. Move on to 100-grit paper to remove the scratch marks left by the 80-grit paper. Don't skip grits.
- Thick, gooey commercial finishes like polyester resin need sanding only to 120 grit. Sand to 180 grit for varnish or lacquer and 220 for oil. Sanding to finer grits is not useful.
- Sand in the direction of the grain. Pay close attention to the wood surface.
- Use the right sandpaper. I use silicon-carbide paper on raw wood; it's gray in color and doesn't clog. Avoid the standard red-colored garnet papers, which clog and don't stay sharp very long. Don't sand with paper that is exhausted.
- Use the right tools. For the projects in this book, you'll need a belt sander, a random-orbit sander, and a palm finishing sander. In addition, a half-sheet finishing sander is useful for large surfaces. You'll also need five sanding blocks (I make these out of scrap wood and attach self-stick sandpaper). Never sand flat surfaces without a tool. Hand-held paper won't flatten the surface.
- Sand by hand when possible. Place a different grit paper in each sanding block (write the grit number on the block), clamp the workpiece, and move quickly through the grits on one surface at a time. Five or ten passes with each grit is plenty. Hand-sanding gives you the most control. You're unlikely to round over edges or make other mistakes because it's much easier to see what you're doing.
- Always wear a dust mask and hearing protection when using sanding machinery. You'll be healthier and more comfortable if you are not breathing in the dust and listening to the din of the sander.

Putting on a top coat

"Top coat" is a generic term for the finish layer, whatever that might be. No matter what finish you choose, putting on a top coat is a three-step process: Put on a couple of coats to seal the wood and raise the grain; sand the finish to flatten it; put on additional coats to build the finish to the depth you want.

Starting with sanded wood, add one layer of top coat. You'll notice that the surface feels rough, like razor stubble, because the grain is raised. Put on a second layer of top coat, or more if necessary, so that when you sand in the next step you won't remove all the finish (this would re-raise the grain, and you'd essentially be starting over again). When using varnish, two coats is usually enough; with thinner top coats, you might need more. Let the finish dry until it is completely hard.

Next, sand the finish flat, taking off all of the stubble. Use a palm or half-sheet finishing sander (not a ROS, which is too aggressive) or a block with 320-grit sandpaper. On carved surfaces such as Queen Anne legs or turnings, sand with paper held in your hand. It won't take long—just a couple of light passes. The surface should feel very smooth and look flat, but you should also still feel finish beneath your fingertips. Don't sand through the finish; if you do, you'll have to start over.

Finally, build top coats until you get the depth of finish you're looking for. There is no right number of coats. Keep building until you're satisfied with the finish—two, three, even five or more coats is not uncommon. You don't need to sand between coats unless you wait a month between coats.

APPENDIX 2: BUYING WOOD

A dining table, with its great expanse of polished wood surfaces, presents a wonderful opportunity for choosing and arranging beautiful pieces of wood or veneer. But before you can select the right material, you have to know where to find it. A beginning woodworker whose local lumberyard offers a choice of clear or knotty pine may regard solid cherry or mahogany, or even sheet goods such as MDF, as exotic materials. Actually, solid hardwoods and sheet goods are readily available in most areas. Living in or near a metropolitan area is helpful but not always necessary for finding high-quality materials. Some of the best lumberyards I know are out in the sticks.

If you have a jointer, planer, and bandsaw, you can buy rough lumber and dimension it—that is, make the faces flat and parallel and make at least one edge flat and perpendicular to the faces. Without these tools, you will have to buy lumber that has already been dimensioned. Lumberyards call this D4S, which stands for "dressed four sides." Sometimes dimensioned lumber has been cut to prespecified lengths such as 6 ft. or 8 ft. Dimensioned lumber is available from some large hardware chain stores and mail-order houses.

You can buy very high-quality wood as dimensioned lumber. However, it is often hard to find boards that match in color or grain. Also, dimensioned lumber is much more expensive than rough lumber. For example, a 1-in. board (called 4/4 and pronounced "four-quarter" in the trade) of dimensioned mahogany at my local hardware store goes for $11 per board foot compared with $3.50 for mahogany in the rough.

Some large lumberyards will dimension rough lumber for you to make what is called D2S, or "dressed two sides," lumber. They do this by putting the boards through a two-headed surface planer, which planes the faces parallel and supposedly joints the boards. However, the jointing is imperfect and can be much worse than that on long boards. Thus, while you may be able to avoid planing the boards, you will still need a jointer to edge-joint. The advantage of using D2S lumber is that you will be able to select the boards you want, matching them for color and grain.

The option that offers the craftsman the most control is buying lumber in the rough and milling it to dimensioned stock. This can be intimidating the first few times you do it. For one thing, you'll need to learn some specialized terminology. For another, rough lumber doesn't even look like a usable product. You can barely see the grain or the color and you have to look closely to pick out knots, cracks, pitch pockets, and other imperfections. However, it's worth learning to do. Using rough lumber gives you the widest selection of species and the biggest selection of stock from which to choose boards.

In large metropolitan areas, look for vendors in the Yellow Pages under hardwoods, lumber, or plywood. In rural areas, you can also look for sawmills that process locally cut trees. Several mills I've visited in rural Pennsylvania also specialize in exotics, importing containers full of ebony or 20-ft.-long logs of bubinga and mahogany. A good sawmill can cut anything from 4/4 boards to large slabs for conference tables.

How Much to Buy

When you buy rough lumber, take into account the waste you will generate in milling it. This varies from one woodworker to another, but I find that I normally need to buy between 1.5 and 1.7 times the required number of finished board feet. For example, if I need 100 bd. ft. of finished dimensioned lumber for a project, I buy 150 bd. ft. to 170 bd. ft. of rough lumber. Sometimes I mark my cuts at the yard, using chalk or crayon, to be sure I will have enough.

Don't buy more lumber than you need for the project you're doing, even if the lumberyard offers you a terrific deal. Lumber takes up a lot of room, which, unless you have a very large space, is better used for tools and projects. Also, there's no guarantee that you'll ever need it again. I have several slabs of bubinga that I got at a good price five years ago. They're beautiful but I should have left them at the lumberyard and let my dealer pay for storing them.

SOURCES OF SUPPLY

CERTAINLY WOOD
13000 Rte. 78
East Aurora, NY 14052-9515
(716) 655-0206
www.certainlywood.com
Veneers, veneer tape

CONSTANTINE'S
1040 E. Oakland Park Blvd.
Ft. Lauderdale, FL 33334
(954) 561-1716
www.constantines.com
Dyed colored veneer for inlay, dimensioned lumber

FLAMINGO SPECIALTY VENEER CO.
356 Glenwood Ave.
East Orange, NJ 07017
(973) 672-7600
www.flamingoveneer.com
Veneer, veneer tape, and other veneering supplies

FORREST MANUFACTURING INC.
457 River Rd.
Clifton, NJ 07014
(800) 733-7111
www.forrest.woodmall.com
High-quality table-saw and circular blades, Hi-AT blades for veneered plywood, sharpening service for all blades

GARRETT WADE
161 Ave. of the Americas
New York, NY 10013
www.garrettwade.com
(800) 221-2942
Forstner bits, mortising chisels and mallets, woodworking tools, finishing supplies, table hardware

HIGHLAND HARDWARE
1045 N. Highland Ave. NE
Atlanta, GA 30306
(800) 241-6748
www.highland-hardware.com
Forstner bits, mortising chisels and mallets, woodworking tools, finishing supplies

LEE VALLEY & VERITAS TOOLS
P. O. Box 1780
Ogdensburg, NY 13669-9973
(800) 267-8735
www.leevalley.com
Mortising chisels, expansion slides, alignment pins, table locks, tabletop fasteners, finishing supplies

OLD FASHIONED MILK PAINT CO.
436 Main St.
Groton, MA 01450
(978) 448-6336
www.milkpaint.com
Milk paint and "Antique Crackle"

ROCKLER WOODWORKING AND HARDWARE
4365 Willow Dr.
Medina, MN 55340
www.rockler.com
(800) 279-4441 (mail order)
(877) 762-5537 (retail locations)
Hardwood dowels, Forstner bits, expansion slides, alignment pins, table locks, tabletop fasteners, tee-nuts and levelers, mortising chisels and mallets, dimensioned lumber

VACUUM PRESSING SYSTEMS, INC.
553 River Rd.
Brunswick, ME 04011
(207) 725-0935
www.vacupress.com
Vacuum pressing bags, pumps, glue spreaders, veneer cutters, resin-impregnated cardboard honeycomb, Unibond 800 urea resin, how-to videotapes on veneer and vacuum pressing, and an Internet forum to ask veneer questions

VAN DYKE'S RESTORERS
P. O. Box 278
Woonsocket, SD 57385
(800) 558-1234
www.vandykes.com
Table hardware, expansion slides

WOODWORKERS SUPPLY
1108 N. Glen Rd.
Casper, WY 82601
(800) 645-9292
Desktop fasteners, tabletop fasteners, expansion slides, alignment pins, table locks, tee-nuts and levelers, readymade aprons, tools, finishing supplies, tenoning jigs, doweling centers

FURTHER READING

Books

Charron, Andy. *Spray Finishing.* Newtown, CT: The Taunton Press, 1996.

Charron, Andy. *Water Based Finishes.* Newtown, CT: The Taunton Press, 1998.

Fine Woodworking on Tables & Desks. Newtown, CT: The Taunton Press, 1986.

Jewitt, Jeff. *Hand-Applied Finishes.* Newtown, CT: The Taunton Press, 1997.

Joyce, Ernest. *Encyclopedia of Furniture Making.* New York: Sterling Publishing, 1987.

Lincoln, William A. *The Complete Manual of Wood Veneering.* Fresno, CA: Lindon Publishing, 1984.

Nagyszalanczy, Sandor. *Fixing and Avoiding Woodworking Mistakes.* Newtown, CT: The Taunton Press, 1995.

Panero, Julius, and Martin Zelnik. *Human Dimension and Interior Space: A Source Book of Design Reference Standards.* New York: Whitney Library of Design/Watson-Guptill Publications, 1979.

Square, David Shath. *The Veneering Book.* Newtown, CT: The Taunton Press, 1995.

Stem, Seth. *Designing Furniture from Concept to Shop Drawing: A Practical Guide.* Newtown, CT: The Taunton Press, 1989 (out of print).

Young, William Tandy. *The Glue Book.* Newtown, CT: The Taunton Press, 1998.

Videotapes

Duginske, Mark. *Mastering Your Bandsaw.* Newtown, CT: The Taunton Press.

Duginske, Mark. *Mastering Woodworking Machines.* Newtown, CT: The Taunton Press.

Mehler, Kelly. *Build a Shaker Table.* Newtown, CT: The Taunton Press.

Mehler, Kelly. *Mastering Your Table Saw.* Newtown, CT: The Taunton Press.

Raffan, Richard. *Turning Wood.* Newtown, CT: The Taunton Press.

Vacuum Pressing Systems. *Working in a Vacuum.* Available directly from Vacuum Pressing Systems, Inc.

Vacuum Pressing Systems. *Working with Veneer.* Available directly from Vacuum Pressing Systems, Inc.

Articles

Graves, Kim Carleton. "Duplicate Spindles by Hand." *Fine Woodworking* 142 (May/June 2000): 68–71.

CONTRIBUTORS

TRESTLE TABLE (P. 40)
Peter S. Turner
Furnituremaker
126 Boothby Ave.
S. Portland, ME 04106
(207) 799-5503
petersturner@hotmail.com

VINEYARD TABLE (P. 56)
Neal White
2446 Nautilus Ct.
San José, CA 95128
(408) 287-2371

EXPANDING RECTANGULAR TABLE (P. 72)
Stephen Brandt
Traditional Woodworks
502 Skyline Rd.
New Cumberland, PA 17070
(717) 770-1118
www.traditionalwoodworks.com
steve@traditionalwoodworks.com

EXPANDING RACETRACK OVAL TABLE (P. 88)
John Lomas
Cotswold Furniture Makers
Sawyer Rd./Box 168
Whiting, VT 05778
(802) 623-8400
cotswold@shoreham.net

EXPANDING PEDESTAL TABLE (P. 106)
Ambrose Pollock
Ambrose Pollock Cabinets, Furniture and Millwork
P. O. Box 22705
Carmel, CA 93922
(831) 624-8145
www.ambrosepollock.com
info@ambrosepollock.com
Gallery showroom: Mission St. between 5th and 6th
Carmel-by-the-Sea, CA 93922
(831) 625-6554

MODERN ROUND TABLE (P. 140)
Kirk Schuly
KS Furniture and Design
446 E. 20th St., Ste. MA
New York, NY 10009
(212) 353-3480
www.kirkschuly.com
kirkschuly@yahoo.com

KITCHEN TABLE (P. 22),
QUEEN ANNE TABLE (P. 122),
BOAT-SHAPED PEDESTAL TABLE (P. 158)
Kim Carleton Graves
Carleton Woodworking
195 Adams St. #8G
Brooklyn, NY 11201
(718) 399-1114
www.CWWing.com
kim@CWWing.com